# MAKING PROFITS

## MALCOLM BIRD

PIATKUS

© Malcolm Bird

First published in 1991 in hardback as
*Improve Your Profits* by
Judy Piatkus (Publishers) Limited
5 Windmill Street, London W1P 1HF

This paperback edition
first published in 1992

**The moral right of the author
has been asserted**

*A catalogue record for this book is available
from the British Library*

ISBN 0-7499-1035-6
ISBN 0-7499-1136-0 (Pbk)

Typeset in 11/13pt Compugraphic Times by
Action Typesetting Limited, Gloucester
Printed and bound in Great Britain by
Biddles Ltd, Guildford and King's Lynn

# MAKING PROFITS

MAKING WORDS

# CONTENTS

# *INTRODUCTION*

Are you the owner or the manager of a small- to medium-sized business?

Whatever the case you will have an interest (to say the least) in the profitability of the enterprise.

You may be chugging along quite nicely and you may be one of that small band of entrepreneurs content to make just enough to 'get by'. It is more likely that even if your business is profitable you are looking for ways to increase those profits – if only to make your business more secure.

In addition, or alternatively, you may want to expand or to diversify into new products or markets and need improved cash flow to do so.

Perhaps you are in a much less happy situation? Are your profits declining? Are interest rates eating away at your business? Are you worried about how to meet your salary bill in a few months' time – or even next month?

It is not likely that some fairy godmother will present you with lower overhead costs in the form of reduced rents or whatever. It is far more likely that you anticipate higher rents, higher insurance costs, a hike in the cost of electricity, gas, water rates and so on. It is also most unlikely that your employees will offer to work for less money – or even be content to forgo a pay increase in the face of inflation and a rising cost of living.

All of this means that you have to be your own fairy godmother and find ways to improve revenue and keep down costs. In short to improve your profits.

Showing you how to do it is the purpose of this book which is based on real-life experience of achieving profit improvement in a variety of businesses and situations.

Some of the actions open to you are of a long-term nature such as going into a new market and developing new customers from scratch. Fortunately, for anyone in a hurry there are some short-term measures which, although not in the nature of a 'quick fix', can start the process with limited delay. Many of these short-term actions are in the cost-saving category and are described in Chapters 3 and 4. Some will make only a small difference but like Mr Micawber's calculation, can make the difference between staying in business or not. Don't be misled into doing nothing about the smaller-cost items simply because they are small – in some cases a minor saving represents the difference between profit and loss or can significantly increase profits in percentage terms.

It is suggested that you work through the various actions and devise a six month plan to improve profits. This could (and perhaps should) start with one or more of the short-term measures and follow through with something longer term. Your programme might comprise, say, an attack on outstanding debts combined with a cost reduction campaign on supplies. These relatively short-term measures could accompany a longer-term look at your products and/or your marketing. The preliminary stages of the longer-term work will probably need to run in parallel with the short-term work. The choice of topics will depend on your circumstances but, whatever the situation, do have a plan with target finishing dates – this will be far more likely to get results than a vague set of good intentions.

Above all, even if you have been content to jog along with a moderate profit can you afford to continue that way? Think about a few 'what ifs?'

- What if a major customer goes bust owing you a lot of money?
- What if your raw material prices suddenly go sky high? If you doubt that this could happen just remember the Gulf Crisis of 1990 and its effect on oil prices and those of associated products.
- What if a competitor launches a new product which beats yours on price, quality or both?

In all these cases you will need cash to cope with the problems. You may have to borrow this cash and your chances of doing so will be proportional to your profit track record.

Even if you have no doubts or fears for the future and you are making a good living from your business, why leave it at that? If you are spending 10 hours a day managing the enterprise, why not get more for your 10 hours of effort? The reward is not just in cash terms. The personal satisfaction in running a highly effective operation is of considerable value to most people in business.

Time – or the lack of it – is an ever-present problem for business people. This has been kept in mind when writing this book. The 'techniques' I describe have been chosen to suit overworked entrepreneurs. They are selected on the basis of yielding the best return on the time spent using them and their relative simplicity.

For convenience the masculine gender has been used throughout the book. Unless the context otherwise indicates, both genders are implied.

# PART ONE

# Standing Back and Looking

# CHAPTER · 1

# PROFIT AND WHERE YOU ARE NOW

Profit is the difference between costs and sales. The difference between current payments and receipts is the cash balance and is very rarely the same as profit.

The cash balance does not take account of items of expense which are as yet unpaid and can also include items such as a provision for bad debts and depreciation of buildings and equipment.

This book is concerned with improving the result of subtracting total costs from the value of sales. Defining profit like this may, at first sight, appear to be rather pedantic, but it is particularly important to the small to medium business. Concentrating on the cash balance and assuming that a healthy cash balance means that all is well is a trap into which many small businesses fall. The chickens tend to come home to roost in a painful way when accrued items such as electricity and gas charges are made and the quarterly rent bill hits the doormat. It is then that it is realised that the real profit is less than the cash position indicated — or that there is no actual profit at all. All of which means that careful budgeting and cash-flow forecasting is a 'must'.

## How can profits be improved?

The answer, of course, is obvious. Or is it?

The obvious answer is that profits can be improved by cutting costs, increasing sales or both. However, as with many things in life, it is not as simple as that. We could, for example, drastically cut costs and *for a time* substantially improve profits. This could involve, say, closing down the telephone sales department, employing lower-grade staff at lower wages, or perhaps cancelling our advertising programme. Any of these would reduce costs but in the medium to long term could so severely reduce sales that the profit position is actually made worse.

Sales could be increased by price reductions. If the price is sufficiently reduced a flood of orders could be produced – followed by a nice fat cash injection. However, this brings us back to the cash balance versus profit question. Certainly the cash balance would improve – temporarily – but the longer-term costs will catch up and could wipe it all out.

The only real ways to improve real profits are:

● To reduce costs without reducing sales revenue – short or long term.
● To increase sales without increasing costs.

Even this is a simplification. It may, for instance, be possible to improve profits by reducing both sales *and* costs.

This can be achieved by eliminating a product which generates revenue insufficient to cover its manufacturing cost, thereby releasing resources to manufacture a product which commands a higher sales price but does not demand higher costs.

Obvious, you may say. No intelligent businessman would continue providing a service or product which costs more to provide than it earns in the market. The fact remains that it happens – frequently.

An instance of the non-profitable product was found in a London financial institution. In this case the 'product' was in fact a service provided to a major foreign client. The company received a substantial fee from the client, who was regarded, and treated, as being of top level importance. For some years this particular client had received personal attention from two of the firm's directors and priority was given to the client's needs.

During the course of an analysis of the business by a management consultant the question of the profitability of the particular client's business was raised. The directors had no doubt that the business was highly profitable. Their surprise (if not disbelief) was complete when a careful examination showed that, despite the size of fee earned, the business was indeed a loss-maker.

The facts uncovered showed quite clearly that the salary cost of the time spent servicing the client's needs exceeded the fees received by a significant margin. This situation had not been obvious to the management because no individual or group was dedicated *solely* to this one client and the total labour cost was hidden.

Some reduction of the cost was achieved by streamlining certain office procedures and cutting out a few frills, but the business concerned continued as non-profitable. For various 'political' reasons the business could not be dropped.

In addition, the business with this client made a contribution to fixed costs – which brings us to another trap for the unwary.

## The contribution to fixed costs trap

Let us imagine a small company making a range of tables and chairs. Assume that one item in the range is a coffee table. The cost of making the coffee table might be, say:

|  | £ |
|---|---|
| Timber | 20.00 |
| Varnish | 1.00 |
| Labour | 25.00 |
| TOTAL | 46.00 |

The table sells at £50.60 yielding a 'profit' of 10%.

However, this will not be the real profit as other costs need to be allowed for, including:

Rent and rates of workshop
Insurances
Cleaning
Transport
Telephone and postage
Office costs, e.g. typing and accounts.

The 10% 'profit' will make a *contribution* to these fixed costs but may not be enough to cover all of them. Each table makes an apparent profit of £4.60, but if the proper share of overheads which should be borne by the coffee tables is, say, £10 then each table makes a loss of £6.40.

The trap in all this is that it is only too easy to assume that if the marginal costs of making one more table (timber, varnish and labour) are covered by the selling price then all is well.

The fact is that *only if there is no other work which can be done* by the employees and other resources should this kind of work be continued with. Even then it should be clearly understood that the work is merely reducing the losses and *not* making a profit.

Getting rid of products like the coffee table is, in effect, reducing gross profit but increasing net profit. It is net profit which counts.

The easiest way to improve profits is to find an item of expenditure which can be reduced or eliminated. That can be easier said than done and is best approached by asking some fundamental questions about the business.

## Where are you now?

The first stage in improving profitability is to take a good hard look at the business. This means standing back and trying to look at it from the viewpoint of a critical outsider. In a sense we will be examining the business in the same way that a consultant would examine it.

The advantage in this 'do-it-yourself' approach is that no consultancy fees have to be paid.

The disadvantage (if that is the right word) is that, unlike a consultant, you may find it difficult to be entirely dispassionate and objective.

## What profit should you be making?

It was pointed out to a businessman that if he shut down his business, realised all the assets and put the money into a secure investment he would be better off – without working at all and with none of the worries of running a business.

The businessman replied, quite understandably, that if he followed this advice he would lose the excitement and other emotional rewards of running his business. He also rightly pointed out that if he gave up he would also abandon all hope of making a really significant profit in the future. The real value to the businessman of the calculations done was in giving him some idea of what profit he *should* be making.

Selling up and investing the proceeds is one guide that can be used. Other indicators are:

- What the owner(s) of the business could earn if they worked for someone else on a salaried or commission basis.
- What profits other similar businesses are making. This is not always easy to find out and it is necessary to be sure that like is being compared with like but despite those difficulties it is worth a shot.

There is, in addition, another very important question to be answered:

## What profit MUST you make?

The owners of a business may be content with a fairly modest return on their capital and the effort they put into the business.

There is even a tendency as people get older to settle for an acceptable life-style and to become complacent about their profit level. This can be a dangerous state of mind.

No business is entirely a matter of the owners' personal wishes or ambitions. Nor does it exist in a sheltered world of its own. The outside world is constantly changing and offering not only opportunities but threats as well. These changes can impose on a business a minimum profit level requirement which is essential for survival.

Recent examples include the 1992 changes in trading between the EC countries and high interest levels in a number of countries. The former can be seen as an opportunity which may require increased liquidity to exploit, the latter as a threat which liquid resources built up from higher profits can fend off.

Another vital requirement for survival is finding *and keeping* dedicated and skilled staff. There is a whole range of actions which management must take to keep its good, indeed essential, people, but one is particularly important. Effective and dynamic people need to see a rewarding future for themselves. Such a future will not be apparent in a static or declining business. Such businesses are likely only to retain the mediocre people and the deadbeats.

A business which makes good profits can more easily afford

research and development of new products, market research to seek opportunities, and the finance for growth. Growth can come from acquisitions as well as from expansion of existing activity. Acquisition, say of an ailing competitor, may need funding from a bank or (preferably) a venture capital company. Such funding will be much easier to obtain if there is a good record of profits from past activities. There is nothing to beat the confidence with which one can approach a potential investor when armed with several years' healthy balance sheets. The potential lender will also be suitably impressed and more willing to put his money at risk.

Other needs which can be met from healthy profits include:

- Replacement of old machinery or equipment.
- Buying in new technology – no later than its purchase by competitors.
- Paying off debenture holders when the due date comes round.
- Taking advantage of a recession.

Recessions in an industry, or across the board, can offer opportunities for the healthy business. Raw materials and other supplies can be bought more cheaply by the company which can pay for them promptly, capital goods may be on offer at attractive prices and markets become easier to penetrate as competitors slow down their activity.

Some or all of these opportunities are available to the company which has achieved a planned profit level essential to survival – or better still a strengthening of its position.

## What size should you be?

This is a question closely related to the profit or turnover point already mentioned. Large size is not necessarily an advantage and no business should blindly seek growth. On the other hand, there can be disadvantages in being too small – most particularly increased vulnerability when the going gets tough (although this is not always the case) and lack of resources to exploit opportunities.

The whole question of size is a difficult one in that the *optimum* size needs to be determined, but the optimum will change as the market and other environmental factors change.

The decision as to whether or not to go for a larger size – or indeed a smaller business – will depend heavily on the judgement of the owners of the business. This judgement must be based on experience and a certain amount of gut-feel.

However, judgement is improved and made more objective by applying some 'techniques'. The first thing to do is to consider the general advantages and disadvantages of growth and size and see to what extent they are applicable to your business.

The advantages of being a bigger fish in the pond are (generally):

● Ability to take on larger contracts.
● Confidence of potential customers in your company; e.g. it is easier to see your product or services if only because you are more likely to be known.
● More clout in purchasing negotiations.
● A larger range of skills among employees – which can enable you to tackle a contract which is slightly different from the normal for your business.
● More clout in negotiating loans or other forms of funding – although this will depend on other factors as well.
● Economies of scale can be enjoyed.
● Normally there will be less dependence on one or two major customers.

The disadvantages of being a bigger fish are (generally):

● Control of the business and the people in it becomes more complicated as numbers increase.
● Co-ordination of activities is more difficult.
● Failure to delegate becomes more and more damaging. By no means all owners are willing to delegate and by no means all know how to do it.

The pros and cons of being a smaller business are mostly the converse of the advantages and disadvantages listed for the larger company. There is however one other aspect which the owners of a small business often find attractive. There is a 'comfort factor' related to size and there are many businessmen who are more comfortable with a small operation. The satisfaction which can be gained from running a business is as important to the individual as the profit. Given that the profit enjoyed is enough to compensate the owners adequately for their efforts and ensure that the business is viable into the future, then why take on the hassle of growth?

There are also individuals who will not be satisfied with a small business and have a burning ambition to be more significant –

even leading personalities – in their industry. For them a plan for growth will be needed.

These personal aspirations should be taken into account in the process of listing the pros and cons of greater or lesser size for your business.

## Looking at your products or services

It is important to avoid the trap of favouring, say, a pet product which has served its purpose and should now be dropped. The battery-operated nail polisher with which you started your company could now be a problem product which is in fact a drain on the business.

A consultant might well tot up all the material, labour and distribution costs of the nail polisher and tell you that it is no longer paying its way. He may also tell you that in the ten years that has elapsed since the product was launched the world has moved on, the market has changed and new types of nail varnish are making the polisher obsolete. This is the kind of fact which must be faced dispassionately. Pouring more money into promoting the nail polisher could be much less rewarding than switching cash and other resources into another of your products or an entirely new one.

In short, you must set aside your emotions and in a hard-headed way answer the questions 'What business are you in?' and 'What business should you be in?'

This could result either in diversification or in abandoning an earlier diversification. The history of business is full of examples such as W. H. Hoover who started in business making leather goods.

## What business are you in?

For many years Marks and Spencer were in the business of selling clothing. The popular perception was of a company providing value-for-money shirts, socks, underwear and the like.

In recent years the perception has changed as Marks and Spencer have changed. They now sell food and furnishings among other additions to their products. In other words, they decided that they were not just in the clothing business but were in the *retail* business – a decision which opened up an almost limitless range of profitable opportunities.

The Marks and Spencer example, along with Boots and Sainsbury's, illustrate how answering the question 'What business are you in?' can open up new vistas. It also shows that a hard look at the business is not limited to disposing of unprofitable products or services.

## Ron and Reg

A small business wrestling with the question at the time of writing is run by Ron and Reg. Finding themselves redundant when a major motor agency folded, the two men set themselves up as a mobile car repair service. After a couple of years they found a workshop and continued the business on a non-mobile basis. They managed the transition with the help of a collection and delivery service – picking up the customer's car from his home and returning it when the work was done. This enabled them to compete in a tough market, as their customers were spared the inconvenience of taking their cars to a workshop themselves and getting back to pick them up before the end of the working day.

The collection service developed, more or less by accident, when some of the customers asked to be dropped off at work, a bus stop or a railway station. The idea grew in the minds of Ron and Reg that a hire car service might pay off. They looked at the competition and decided that it could work.

This proved to be the case. After a further three years the hire car service is doing very well and has the advantage over the repair service that expensive stocks of spares are not required and other items such as workshop rent, rates and heating are avoided.

Now, a hard look at the business as a whole has raised the question, 'Are we in the car repair business or the car hire business?'

It is likely that Ron and Reg will put more time and resources into car hire and gradually wind down the repair side to the point where they only service their own fleet of cars. The result is expected to be a higher overall profit and less reliance on the bank to finance stock holding and other costs. Having accepted that currently they are in the car repair *and* car hire service they are now considering the question 'What business *should* we be in?'

The process of answering the two questions is made easier and more disciplined by following three steps. If followed thoroughly and with brutal honesty, the most promising future direction for the business is almost certain to emerge.

## Step 1 – Defining the parts of the business

Even the smallest business can be broken down into parts. The village post office is likely, in addition to providing postal and related services, to have a small retail side. Typically, the shop side of the business will provide stationery, small toys and even items of clothing.

These parts of the business must be isolated to be examined separately at a later stage.

A small manufacturer may have only one product but the business can be examined on the basis of various functions such as purchasing, manufacture and sales.

Sometimes manufacturing is accompanied by some form of service or, in the case of a service-only company, a range of add-ons to the mainstay of the business. Examples are printers who may offer a design service or a travel agency which may provide help in obtaining visas.

Once the various bits and pieces of your business have been clearly identified – and it takes a lot more thought than appears at first sight – you can move on to step 2.

## Step 2 – Measuring the parts

As far as is humanly possible, each part of the business should now be measured in terms of its contribution to profitability. This is not always straightforward since many costs such as heating and lighting will be shared. It is difficult in many cases to allocate these shared costs with great accuracy. Fortunately a very high degree of accuracy is not necessary as an 'order of magnitude figure' will normally suffice. The aim should be to clarify the relative importance of the various parts of the business to the overall operation.

In cases where there is clearly only one definable product or service the relative costs of the functions such as purchasing and sales can be ascertained. The result is often a raised eyebrow at one or other of the costs and some enthusiasm for a closer look.

Quite a lot of business people find it difficult quickly to answer questions such as 'What does your sales operation cost you?' or 'How does your distribution cost compare with your production cost?'

If the answer is that distribution costs more than production, then there may well be a need to examine the distribution method in some detail.

## Checklist of activities worth costing out

*Office procedures*
Design
Job costing
Quotations
Book keeping
Invoicing
Purchasing
Payroll
Stock records
Order entry
Production planning
Mailing

*Marketing*
Sales force
Advertising
Exhibiting
Samples

*Production and distribution*
Machine maintenance
Machine utilisation
Stock control
Transporting
Testing
Packaging
Progress chasing

## Step 3 – Coming up with some conclusions

Having analysed the various parts of the business some conclusions must be reached. You may decide that the situation is entirely satisfactory, that there are no opportunities to be exploited or problems to be tackled. It is much more likely that something somewhere will need a decision.

For example:

● Is there an add-on service which costs more than it is worth?
  We often say that our only edge over the competition is our
  level of service. This is often true but not always. The value of
  the service to our business is actually the value placed on it by
  our customers. What is their viewpoint? Do they *really* value
  the service highly? Would they go elsewhere if the service was
  removed or reduced?

  One way to find out is to ask them − a process which
  sometimes produces some surprising answers.

● Could additional modest capital investment lead to improved
  profitability? For example, a small and relatively inexpensive
  machine may remove a bottleneck in a production line and
  increase output rates. This is a common situation found in
  both offices and factories or workshops. The full capacity of
  a number of interdependent facilities is not utilised because
  one of them is inadequate. This is the old 'weak link in the
  chain' syndrome.

  Examples from real life include:

  − Installing an 'automatic' saw-bench in a small factory.
    Output was more than doubled when the saw-bench was
    introduced − at a capital cost of only £1500.

  − The use of a word processor to produce standard letters,
    and documents with variable clauses in an insurance office.
    The output of the office had been dominated entirely by the
    speed at which a typist could depress keys on her typewriter.

● Could investment in more labour have a beneficial effect? It
  normally goes against the grain to increase the wage bill when
  looking for ways to improve profits. However, like the case
  with machines it is not uncommon to find the output of a
  skilled employee − or a group of employees − slowed down
  by the need to carry out time-consuming low-level tasks. If
  some of the work is unskilled and can be undertaken by a
  cheaper and unskilled person, the net result could be more
  profit − despite the increase in the total wage bill.

● Are there any underemployed people? Are there any jobs
  which are not essential, or which could be done more cheaply
  by a sub-contractor?

21

- Is there an opportunity to charge for a service which perhaps started in a small way, is provided free and is now growing?

- Can we develop an add-on service into a prime revenue earner? In other words, make the service a revenue earner in its own right?

- Are there any opportunities for cost reduction? It is most unlikely that there are none at all and the whole of Part Two of this book is dedicated to ways and means to save money.

- Are there any products or services which are becoming more and more of a problem?

  Difficulties in finding the right kind of raw materials or suitably trained staff, creeping obsolescence or simply increased competition can cause a hitherto valuable product to become a problem. If this is so you may be flogging a dying horse and wasting money trying to keep it going.

  There may, at the same time, be an opportunity which is being neglected and it could well be a good move to switch resources from the problem to the opportunity.

- Is the business suffering from overtrading? Fast growth leads to a need for more and more cash to finance the expansion. This often means more and more expensive borrowings. It could be better to go for a more modest rate of growth (or a period of non-expansion) to improve margins rather than turnover. A profit of 10% on a £1,000,000 turnover is better than 1% on a £5,000,000 turnover.

- Are there any highly speculative projects which should be abandoned – regardless of how much has been spent on them?

  Having spent a lot of money there is a natural reluctance to admit that a project is likely to be a failure and to cut one's losses by bringing it to an end. Having the courage and commonsense to do so could, in the worst cases, prevent the firm going bust.

  Conversely we may have spent a lot of money on a development which needs just a bit more to complete it. The accountants are probably sounding severe warnings and advising pulling out. Provided that you feel confident of a successful future it may well be better to press on. If, for example, you have spent £50,000 on developing your frictionless bearing but need a further £10,000 to complete it then the question to be asked is: 'Is it worth paying £10,000 for a frictionless bearing?' The £50,000 already spent has gone forever and cannot be recovered; but there is no logic in abandoning the project if you have every reason to expect it to be a winner.

● Are there ways in which revenue can be improved in a way which contributes to profits? Perhaps the obvious and first possibility is an increase in selling price – often a step too long delayed by small businesses due to fear of losing customers. This and other ways to increase revenue is examined in Part Three.

All these questions, and no doubt others which may suit your particular business, should be answered dispassionately and then used as a basis for a plan for the future. A plan which should be aimed at a profit objective.

## SUMMARY OF KEY POINTS

1. Profit should not be confused with the cash balance. This book is concerned with the true profit – the difference between costs and sales revenue.

2. There are a number of ways to improve profits but some of these are traps for the unwary.

3. It is not unheard of for a business which is firmly believed to be profitable to be, in reality, loss-making – with one or more products or services merely making a contribution to fixed costs and not actually profitable.

4. Work out what profit you should be making and what you *must* make.
   How does this compare with what is happening and what the future is likely to hold if you continue as before?

5. Decide what size your business should be. List the pros and cons of growth (or shrinkage) in the context of your industry, your market and what you and your employees want out of life.

6. Take care to be objective when reviewing your business. Don't allow your past pet products, customers or whatever to cloud your judgement as to the realities of the situation now.

7. Be clear about what business you are in. Exclude activities which are not truly appropriate, but consider the widest range of activity which lies within the definition of your business.

8. To define the business you are in, break it down into parts and then measure each one in some suitable way e.g. cost, revenue contribution, management time – or whatever gives you a way to assess the cost/value of the various activities.

9. Ask yourself some tough and searching questions about your findings. In particular, which aspects of the business present problems and which present opportunities?

# CHAPTER 2

# SOME TECHNIQUES TO HELP YOU PLAN AHEAD

## Break-even point calculations

There are always costs which must be met, regardless of the level of activity. These, the fixed costs, are normally made up of rent and other expenses related to buildings plus wage costs. Wage costs in the medium to long term may be variable to some extent, but generally speaking it is neither possible nor desirable to hire and fire as work goes up or down.

The variable costs (such as the timber and varnish for the coffee table mentioned in Chapter 1) are those items which are directly related to the level of production. The relationship between fixed and variable costs and the size of the business in terms of turnover are important factors to take into account in your review of the business. They are also a factor which will, at least in part, determine your profitability. There will be an existing relationship based on present levels of activity and it is important to calculate what the relationship will be if output is reduced or if you go for growth.

The calculation is illustrated by the following example:

a.   Assume that a company is currently producing 1000 stapling machines per month.

b.   Assume that there are 5 employees each paid £1000 per month.

c.   Assume that the rent and other fixed costs are £500 per month.

d.   Assume that the variable cost of each stapler (metal, springs etc.) is £1.

Given these figures it is possible to enter them into a table showing what the costs add up to for varying levels of production:

| No. of Staplers | Fixed Cost | Variable Cost | Total Cost | Cost per Stapler |
|---|---|---|---|---|
| | £ | £ | £ | £ |
| 700 | 1500 | 700 | 2200 | 3.14 |
| 800 | 1500 | 800 | 2300 | 2.87 |
| 900 | 1500 | 900 | 2400 | 2.66 |
| 1000 | 1500 | 1000 | 2500 | 2.50 |
| 1100 | 1500 | 1100 | 2600 | 2.36 |
| 1200 | 1500 | 1200 | 2700 | 2.25 |
| 1300 | 1500 | 1300 | 2800 | 2.15 |

Suppose that the going rate in the market for a stapler is £6.00. At the present output of 1000 staplers the business is making a profit of $1000 \times (6.00 - 2.50) = £3500$ per month.

You can see that if you can increase production (and sales) to 1300 staplers a month the profit would be $1300 \times (6.00 - 2.15) = £5005$.

However, if you discover that to reach this level of output you must take on 1 more employee *and* another unit of factory space the result will be very different. If the new employee adds £1000 to the fixed costs and the factory unit another £500, then the cost calculation for 1300 staplers is:

| Fixed Cost | Variable Cost | Total Cost | Cost per Stapler |
|---|---|---|---|
| £ | £ | £ | £ |
| 3000 | 1300 | 4300 | 3.31 |

The profit from selling 1300 staplers would be $1300 \times (6.00 - 3.31) = £3497$.

This is less than the profit made with an output of only 1000 per month and you have not even taken into account the extra effort of selling 300 more staplers or the additional supervision required by the new employee.

The important point to note is that although fixed costs remain static over a considerable range of output levels, when they go up they go up with a bang. This can easily mean that a growing company will go from periods of profit into periods of loss until, having reached a yet higher level of production, it will once again emerge into a profitable period.

Further growth if combined with yet another hike in fixed costs can bring the business back into a loss-making position.

The relationship between costs and profits is often shown by a graph such as in Figure 1.

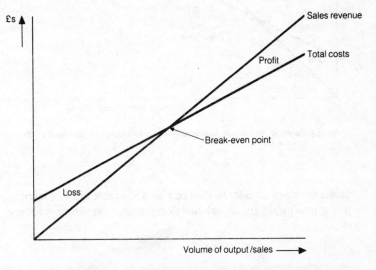

Figure 1. The traditional graph showing cost and profit relationships at varying levels of output.

According to this graph, as production increases from zero the loss will diminish until break-even point is reached – after which a profit will be achieved. This is only true if fixed costs remain constant for all levels of production. In real life the situation is likely to be different, as illustrated in Figure 2.

In this case break-even point I is reached and a profit achieved – until the fixed costs suddenly rise causing an abrupt increase in total costs. It is now necessary to pass break-even point II before a profit can be made.

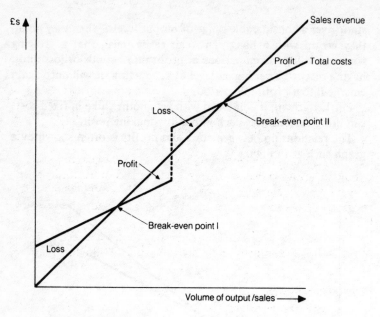

Figure 2. The actual effect of fixed cost increase on the cost and profit relationship at varying levels of output.

Some break-even calculations can be a valuable aid to planning a more profitable future when taking a look at where you are now.

## An 80:20 analysis

Another simple but potentially very informative technique is the 80:20 analysis.

This technique is derived from Pareto's Principle which, in ordinary English, states that there is a tendency for a few components of a range of items to be responsible for most of the value.

This can mean, for example, that:

● 20% of the customers account for 80% of the company income; or
● 80% of the manufacturing costs are attributable to 20% of the product range; or

- 80% of the cost of holding stock is accounted for by 20% of the items in the warehouse; or
- 80% of a manager's time is taken up by only 20% of his responsibilities.

Of course, the ratio is not likely to be exactly 80:20 in real life. The principle holds good, however, that a few items or transactions or whatever will dominate the situation.

In one real-life case, approximately 80% of the cost of stock holding in an engineering spares store was accounted for by 11 spare electric motors. The rest of the stock was made up of dozens of packets of washers, nuts and bolts and other low-value items.

On realising this fairly obvious but hitherto overlooked situation, the company could take advantage of the fact that:

**a.** Time-consuming efforts to keep down stock-holding costs by controlling the level of the bits and pieces was largely ineffectual.

**b.** Reducing the number of spare motors (which was not difficult) resulted in a significant saving.

Making the saving on stock holding costs brought instant joy to the company accountant, and a more relaxed attitude to the nuts and bolts made the storekeeper's life easier.

Carrying out an 80:20 analysis can provide valuable guidance as to where savings can be made. The analysis can also direct management attention towards products and markets which offer opportunities and away from problems areas.

In real-life cases 80:20 analyses have revealed that:

- Most of the short-term absenteeism was concentrated in one department.
- Most of the free samples and other expensive 'extras' were related to one sales region — and hence one salesman.
- The bulk of the costs caused by slow payers were caused by a minority of customers all of the same type.

Some people claim that an analysis should not be necessary to be aware of such information. But the gut-feel approach does not always work and the results of taking a formal look at the situation can result in surprises – pleasant or otherwise. It is also a fact that the manager who is generally aware that something is 'out of proportion' will do little about it until the actual figures are worked out. Seeing the numbers can result in some very useful action.

## Where are you on the life cycle?

Businesses, like living things, have a life cycle. The life cycle can be broadly divided into four phases, illustrated in Figure 3.

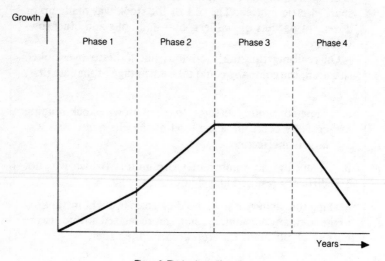

Figure 3. The business life cycle.

In phase 1 the business has a small share of the market but is growing at a fair rate. During phase 2 the business, having survived the hazardous early years, is becoming established and is rapidly increasing its share of the market. Phase 3 is reached when a large share of the market has been gained but growth is now small – or nil. Phase 4 is characterised by a falling share of the market leading to the ultimate demise of the business.

It may seem incorrect or even bizarre to liken businesses in this way to living things. There is, however, enough historical evidence to show that, *unless something is done about it* by management, a business will mirror the development of, say, a human being. The initial stages of life – the first five or six years – are similar to the vulnerable years of a human infant. Later, both will grow stronger at a high rate until, like the human being around 20 years of age, a long period of relative stability will set in. The human being eventually and inevitably reaches phase 4 and gradually deteriorates until he finally goes to that great market in the sky.

Phase 4, as will be explained, is *not* inevitable for a business — but positive action must be taken to avoid it.

First, though, let us look at the characteristics of a business in the various phases. By using these characteristics you can identify the point on the life cycle which your company has reached and take the necessary action to avoid trouble.

## Phase 1

This is the entrepreneurial stage when the company is often driven by a single founder/proprietor.

The business will be:

- Creative. The proprietor and perhaps one or two close associates will be full of ideas and will try out new products or services with limited prior debate and hesitation.
- Customer oriented/driven. A few customers will provide the orders and the business will react to their needs and organise activities accordingly.
- Aggressive. Perceived opportunities, however slight, will be followed up vigorously and corners will be cut to provide a product that someone wants. Selling will be opportunistic and determined.
- The management style will be highly individual — following the personality of the owner of the business or, if there are more than one, the personality of the most dominant.

  At the same time there will be a high degree of informality. Small numbers of employees and the closeness of the management to what is going on will mean that communication is ad hoc and such things as job descriptions or planning meetings will not be used.

## Phase 2

The business is now established and has grown to a point where it can no longer be adequately managed by one person who makes all the decisions.

A team system will have developed in which the more senior people (perhaps 3 or 4) will have delegated powers and contribute to strategic thinking and decisions.

The business will:

- Be market-oriented rather than customer-oriented. There will be less dependence on a few customers and response will be to a perceived *market* demand.
- Use a more strategic and longer-range approach rather than week-to-week tactical thinking.
- Use formal controls including such measures as output and cost reports to management, stock and consumption records, fairly detailed budgeting and controls on employees such as job descriptions and time-keeping records.
- Be changing. Innovation will be welcomed by management, e.g. in response to market needs. Working methods and product design will be reviewed and, if it is considered desirable, changed.

## Phase 3

In this phase the business is considered to be safely established and management methods have become formal.

The characteristics will include:

- A degree of complacency. Up-and-coming competition − or even new and threatening technology − will be viewed with some disdain. Management will feel secure behind a satisfactory balance sheet and a regular flow of orders.
- Very stable structures. There is likely to be a pyramid-shaped organisation which changes very little and rarely in any significant way. Departments will go on in the same way and as part of the same reporting structure for many years − and no one will challenge the arrangement.
- A high level of formality. Approval for expenditure, for instance, will follow a rigid procedure as will such things as promotions, transfers and research.

  Status symbols in the form of company cars, size and opulence of offices, and perks of various kinds will be well established − not least being the eating facilities, which will be graded from works canteen (pies and chips) to directors' dining room (Boeuf à la mode and Château Lafitte).

● Lots of analysis. Management at all levels will be involved in analyses of everything in sight from car park utilisation to fuel consumption in company lorries and from canteen costs to raw material wastage.

   Much of the analysis will be practical, realistic and useful. Unfortunately, a good deal will be pointless and even misleading. Phase 3 is one in which many businesses fall prey to the danger of 'paralysis by analysis'. Entrepreneurial attitudes have now virtually disappeared (probably suppressed) and any intended innovation is swamped by an obsession with obtaining and dissecting more and more statistics before making a decision.

● A stable product line. Products will remain constant in terms of design and mix over long periods and will probably change only in response to external factors such as the success of a competitor. The business will be more of a follower in the market than a leader. Innovation and diversification will be re-active rather than pro-active.

● Developing mediocrity. The complacency of top management and unwillingness to be pro-active will result in an environment which discourages the more energetic and imaginative employees. People with ideas will be positively discouraged and proposals for change rejected or delayed into infinity.

   Gradually, middle management will be made up of mediocre people who are happier to work in a non-demanding business and are content to do as they are told. The more lively and ambitious people will move on, leaving the mediocre behind.

## Phase 4

When this phase is reached the business is on the way down – and out. Market share will be falling. Income will also be falling whilst overheads will remain unchanged. Thus, profits will be going down.

   The business will be characterised by:

● A wholly reactive management which acts on an expediency basis and lurches from one crisis to another.
● Mediocrity (and apathy) will be well entrenched at all levels.

33

- Sacred cows will be much in evidence and demonstrated by such comments as:
  - 'It is not our policy to . . .'
  - 'The M.D. will not countenance the use of computerised systems.'
  - 'The self-lubricating widget is the bed-rock of our business and must not be altered in any way.'
  - 'We never do business in the Far East.'
  - 'Employees are never permitted to . . .'
- An introverted attitude. Very little time will be spent looking at the market for the company products or services. A lot of time will be spent examining the company navel in great detail. The most trivial internal matters will be endlessly discussed at top level whilst events in the market will be neglected.
- An out-of-date and unexciting product line – many products being sacred cows.

## How long does all this take?

Unlike human beings, whose life cycle is still working out around the biblical three score years and ten, the company life cycle is widely variable in length. One London-based company reached phase 4 after about 120 years. Another, in the same line of business, reached it after only 12 years. The reasons for the differences in length are many and varied.

Much will depend on the personality and management style of the leaders of the business and their willingness – combined with ability – to make changes of the right kind.

There must be a readiness to face facts and to accept that change is needed – even if this means killing off some sacred cows – in order to re-activate the business which has reached a plateau.

Fortunately, death is not inevitable and phase 4 of the life cycle can be postponed, perhaps indefinitely.

## Postponing Phase 4

The company which has reached phase 3 must look for ways to return to the characteristics of phase 2. This will not necessarily be easy but will be much more achievable than converting from phase 4 to phase 2.

There may be a number of ways to achieve the switch, including:

- A re-vamped product line.
- Bringing in new managers who are not bogged down by the traditions, phobias and obsessions of the past.
- Clearing out all the bureaucratic paraphernalia.
- Retraining all levels of management to bring about a higher level of managerial skill and to change attitudes.
- A combination of some of the above.

Let us take as an illustration a relatively simple, hypothetical situation which is familiar in real life.

Imagine a company making only one product – a detergent called 'Washo'.

Washo was launched onto the market five years ago with lots of effective publicity and a well prepared, highly motivated sales force. During the first two years Washo steadily won an increasing market share and in the second two years became dominant. Now, after a further year, Washo has a high but static share of the market.

The managment of the company have recognised that Washo is now vulnerable. If a competitor enters the field with a new and more exciting product, then Washo could lose its dominance and go into a rapid decline. A change is needed to bring Washo back into a growth phase. The objective is to change the life cycle graph as shown in Figure 4.

The company's decision to change the product and introduce Washo II with magical bio-ingredient restores demand for the company's output and extends its period of growth. The management, realising that the day will come when Washo II will reach a plateau is now planning its next change – 'Green Washo, the environment friendly detergent'.

By means of a series of changes, either to products or something else, a business can avoid or shorten its phase 3 plateau and prevent itself from entering phase 4. Even if phase 4 is reached, a recovery is by no means impossible – even if more difficult.

This has been illustrated in recent years by a number of successful management buyouts which have resulted in a

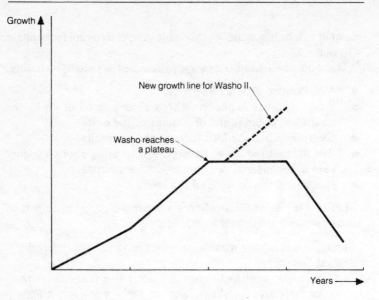

Figure 4. Returning to phase 2 by introducing Washo II.

revitalised business and a return to fast growth and improved profits.

There is, of course, a financial restraint on what a business can do to bring about a new rate of growth or level of profit. No business will have access to unlimited funds and it is vital to ensure that provision is made for the essentials of survival. This means good budgeting.

## What does the company budget look like?

Perhaps your first question should be: 'Do we work to a budget at all?' Many small companies prepare cash-flow forecasts – often because the bank manager insists on it. Less attention may be paid to the company budget, which is in essence a plan for expenditure.

The value of a budget lies in the fact that in order to prepare it a company must, at least once in a year, take a good look at itself and decide what it needs to spend its money on.

Funds available from reserves and/or income will be allocated and this provides an opportunity to decide which items of expenditure will be most important in terms of profit.

It may be better to:

36

● Reduce expenditure on company cars and put more money into advertising.
● Postpone refurbishment of the offices and put funds into new machinery.
● Prepare for a modification of a product or products rather than extend the warehouse; etc.

A good look at the budget can yield dividends, especially if we repeatedly ask the question: 'How does this item of expenditure contribute (directly or indirectly) to profits?'

Conversely, you should consider whether profits are being damaged by neglecting investment in some aspect of the company's operations. At all events such an exercise should ensure that money is wisely (i.e. profitably) spent and that opportunities are not lost.

You may be satisfied that the budget has been well prepared and that the best use of company funds has been identified and agreed. If so, the next thing to look at is how well or badly the budget has been adhered to. It is always possible to find a reason (sometimes a good one) for not sticking to the budget and it is always possible to have such inadequate expenditure controls that the budget is breached inadvertently. The fact is that a lot of discipline is required and divergence from the budget should be treated as a major issue.

At all costs avoid the trap of changing the budget whenever it is convenient to do so. This step is not unknown, and it makes the whole exercise a nonsense.

## Some swotting – the penultimate step

Having looked at various aspects of the business using the breakeven technique, the 80:20 rule or other methods, the various facts and conclusions which have emerged can be put together in a SWOT analysis. Such an analysis means taking a look at the business under four headings:

Strengths
Weaknesses
Opportunities
Threats

The result should be a summary of your overall look at the business which will point you in the direction you should go to improve future profits.

The result could look something like this:

## Strengths

1. Well-trained production staff.
2. Good reputation for service.
3. Two established products with an expected life exceeding 3 years.
4. Cash flow under control.
5. No imminent increase to fixed costs expected.

## Weaknesses

1. Production planning inadequate.
2. Poor sales results in Southern area. 90% of sales to only 10% of customers − which means that the loss of only one or two could be serious.
3. Three products showing no increase in sales. One product showing a fall in sales.
4. Semi-finished stock levels high and rising − mainly for the products with stable sales rates. These account for 65% of stock cost and are the result of poor production planning.
5. Budget for administrative costs repeatedly exceeded. General lack of financial control.
6. Bad debts up by 25% over previous year.

## Opportunities

1. Reliable market information indicating that the demand for coloured widgets will rise.
2. Removal of trade barriers to East European countries.

## Threats

1. Bank pressing for reduction in overdraft.
2. Interest rates expected to rise during the next 6 months.
3. Major competitor increasing sales effort in Southern area.

The results of the SWOT analysis should give some fairly clear indication of what needs to be done both long and short term. These needs can now be translated into the final results of your look at the business.

## Swot analysis – some aspects to look at

*Staff*
Skills
Enthusiasm
Age distribution (will a number of skilled people retire at the same time?)
Potential

*Machinery and Equipment*
Age and condition
Age and obsolescence
Running costs
Operator skills needed
Output rates

*Finances*
Cash resources and revenue
Overdraft and other external financing
Debtors and creditors
Financial standing e.g. credit rating
Fixed and variable costs
Price and cost trends

*Product or service*
Age and design
Life expectancy
Mix of products
Quality standards

*The market place*
Present and future size of market
Competition now and expected
Trends e.g. in customer preferences (how green is your product?)
Selling methods
Service standards
Demographic factors

# A plan for action

Yes, a plan for the future is necessary. Lack of a plan means that you will live from day to day responding to the priorities of the moment – and will continue to be vulnerable to the threats. In addition, strengths and opportunities are unlikely to be fully exploited (if at all) and weaknesses will remain as weaknesses. This means that if your competitors only half get their act together your business could go to the wall.

The plan should be as concise as possible and realistic. Everything in the plan should be relevant and achievable even if with some difficulty.

Based on the SWOT analysis already described, the plan might be along these lines:

## A  Production and production planning

● Joe Snatchet, production planner, to be formally trained in production planning techniques and a review of the present planning system to be carried out by the Production Manager. This to be completed by 1 October.

● Stock levels to be reduced to 50% of present levels and afterwards monitored on a twice-weekly basis by the production planner. This to be completed by 31 December.

● The product with a falling sales record to be phased out and resources switched to developing a coloured widget. Prototypes to be ready for testing by 1 November. Person responsible – Production Manager.

## B  Sales

● Products with an expected life exceeding 3 years to be supported by a promotion budget increase equal to the amount provided hitherto to the product to be phased out.

  The sales manager will prepare a revised advertising campaign to be implemented during the period October – December.

● A detailed examination of Southern area sales will be carried out by the sales manager. The capabilities of the area sales representative to be enhanced with a refresher training course and a target list of new customers to be prepared. These items to be completed by 1 October and a campaign to improve sales launched to coincide with the advertising campaign during October, November and December.

● A study to be made by the MD of potential markets in the East European countries identifying the most favourable target country for our products – and which products will have the greatest demand. This to be completed by 1 November and to be followed immediately by a production/sales plan to exploit the possibilities.

## C  Finance

● Improved liquidity resulting from reduction of stock levels and any improvement in sales revenue to be used to reduce the level of bank overdraft by 10% by year end. A further reduction of 10% to be aimed for during the first six months of next year. Person responsible – Accountant.

● A review will be undertaken of all administrative costs. Ways and means to reduce expenditure in the following areas will be sought by Mr Bloggs:

- Stationery supplies.
- Telephone, telex and facsimile.
- Use of company vehicles.
- Postage and carrier services.
- Electricity and water tariffs.
- Computer services.
- Vending machines.
- Office and workshop cleaning.

All supply contracts are to be reviewed and wherever possible renegotiated. Wastage levels to be reduced and non-essential purchases discontinued. An overall reduction of 12% to be achieved by 31 January.

A plan such as this will help to ensure that some positive action will take place as a result of the review of the company affairs.

The plan, to be effective, must state what is to be done in measurable terms such as 'a 50% reduction' or 'a 10% increase'. Without a specific figure nothing much will happen. If, for example, the plan merely says 'increase sales in the Southern area', then the target will be achieved by a minute increase. A clear, defined and measurable target is essential. This target should, in addition, be *calculated*. Some arbitrary figure snatched out of the air by the MD could be meaningless and not in line with other targets. If, for example, we are aiming to reduce the overdraft by 10%, then that precise amount of money must become available as a result of action targeted in sales production or whatever. Any additional expenditure that is planned, e.g. on training, product development or equipment, must also be allowed for in the equation.

It is also essential clearly to state in the plan *who* is responsible for the various actions agreed upon. If this is not done there will at best be a muddle and at worst nothing will happen, as everyone will find a good reason for saying 'I thought you were doing that' or 'No one told me to do it'.

Finally, the plan should state who will monitor and co-ordinate the implementation. It could well be the case that some actions will be entirely successful while others will be only partly successful – or even a dismal failure. Corrective action, or a change of plan, may be necessary and someone must be in overall charge to mastermind the package as a whole.

Giving some extra help in a weak area or modifying the plan in the light of events should not be regarded as a sign of failure. Rarely will things go exactly as hoped – if only because uncontrollable external influences will play a part. These can include such things as:

- The weather.
- Action of competitors.
- Strikes e.g. at a major supplier.
- A flu epidemic.
- A change in tax law.

## Communicating the plan

It is not enough to communicate the plan, its details and purpose to a few key people. The full co-operation of everyone from the office boy to the MD will be required. Employees who do not know what is intended *and why* cannot be expected either to be enthusiastic about changes which affect them or to act intelligently (e.g. in conformity with the plan) in the course of their day-to-day activities. All employees must be committed, and communication is necessary to achieve this. The alternative could be mistrust and irritation.

The overall strategy should be fully explained and the various steps to be taken described in detail. Once this has been done the various actions can be started.

## SUMMARY OF KEY POINTS

1.  Work out some break-even points for various scenarios. This will help you to reach objective conclusions.

2.  Try an 80:20 analysis to pinpoint significant aspects of the business and to indicate opportunities such as cost saving.

3.  Take a look at the general nature of your business and compare it with those attributes which can tell you where you are in the company life cycle. If you can see evidence of being in phase 3 or phase 4, do something – now.

4.  Have a good hard look at your budget. Are there any major shifts in emphasis which should be made?

5.  Try a SWOT analysis as another way to point you in the right future direction.

6.  After your thorough and objective look at the business, prepare a *plan* for future activity based on your findings and conclusions. Don't forget to communicate the plan – to everyone.

# PART TWO

# Cutting Costs

CHAPTER · **3**

# *REDUCING THE COST OF DEBTS AND LOANS*

The first thing you must do is reduce the cost of your borrowing. If your business is borrowing from a bank at, say, 15% interest and you are in turn waiting an average of 78 days to be paid by your customers, then you are losing a lot of money.

Seventy-eight days is a calculation of the *average* payment period in the United Kingdom based on surveys carried out in 1989. Although this means that some companies are being paid more quickly some of the time, some are being paid even later than 78 days some of the time.

Typical of what this delay can cost is the bank interest of £1060 paid to fund a debt due to a small company and delayed for just under six months. If payment had been made at 30 days – as originally agreed – the borrowing cost to the supplying company would have been about £200. This is bad enough but the additional £860 underlines the need for positive ways and means to *prevent* the problem in the first place.

## Prevention – the cheapest solution

Keeping the cost of overdue debts to the minimum starts not with the customer's accounts payable department but within your own business. A significant percentage of the delay can be self-inflicted and results from lack of agreed procedures and controls, often combined with a straightforward lack of attention to the question of getting the money in. Clinching another deal or completing an important production run are likely to be much more exciting and impressive than dealing with the paperwork. The sad fact is that, no matter how brilliant everything else may be, the only end result which counts is the banking of the customer's cheque. In the worst of all cases you may not be paid at all. What then is required?

## 1. Do some checking before you accept the order
Asking for references and making some enquiries before accepting an order from an individual or company you do not know is a 'must'.

Don't be influenced by the *size* of the order. It is only too easy to become excited by a large order and to assume that because it is large the customer can and will pay.

Your bank can (for a fee) provide a report on the financial status of a company, or there are agencies specialising in this kind of work who can be used. Possibly more valuable, if you have them, are contacts in the trade. A telephone call to someone with experience of the company you are checking out can be very revealing.

## 2. Formally agree the terms of payment
Nothing should be left to chance – or to purely oral agreement. If for instance you have completed a discussion with the customer and agreed what is to be supplied and how payment is to be made, put it in writing. It is a good idea to write out the terms of payment in the customer's presence and for each of you to have a copy. The details can be incorporated in a contract later (if you use one) but at least you have put the customer on notice that you are businesslike and pay proper attention to being paid. This will almost certainly influence his actions when he receives your invoice.

Every effort should be made to incorporate in the terms those factors which will bring forward payment. These might include:

● *Money up front*
  This is an ideal arrangement if only because *you* can earn interest on the money while you are fulfilling the customer's needs. Whatever the size of the payment it also limits your risk in the event that your customer goes bust before the transaction is completed. You will at least have *some* payment for your effort.

  Don't be afraid to ask for money in advance – the chance of losing the order as a result is probably less than you think.

- *Stage payments*
  Ask for payments as clear stages of a deal are concluded. Suppose for example you are supplying a computer system including hardware, software and various services. Payments, proportional to the value of the completed stages, could be asked for when:

  **a.** Systems design is complete.
  **b.** Hardware is delivered.
  **c.** Hardware is installed and tested.
  **d.** Software is tested.
  **e.** Training of staff is completed.
  **f.** System goes live.

  The customer is being asked only to pay for what he has actually received and you are avoiding the costs of funding a deal which could take many months to bring to a conclusion.

- *Discounts for prompt (or early) payment*
  This is an arrangement to be conceded with some care. It should not be forgotten that offering, say, 5% discount for paying 30 days earlier is the equivalent of about 60% per year. Such rates of discount are better received than given, but you can, if the market allows, build them into your pricing structure. There are quite a lot of people who will pay early to gain a discount and it could be a good move if you get your arithmetic right.

- *A price reduction for a second order*
  This amounts to a delayed discount but has the advantage of encouraging further business.
  The customer is offered a lower price for a further order *if* he pays within, say, 30 days for the first order.

### 3. Make sure that you have a system
Your own method for preparing and sending out invoices can be a major contribution to delays in being paid. Each day that passes before the invoice is despatched will cost you something, if it is only the interest you would have enjoyed if you had received the payment and put it into a building society account. In the meantime, your customer may be enjoying the interest.
  Rule number one, therefore, is to organise yourself so that as

soon as is practicable after fulfilling the order an invoice is mailed to the customer.

Ideally, a standard should be laid down, say 48 hours, as the time allowed to complete and mail the invoice. The use of a word processor can be a great help in that the bulk of the invoice – and certainly any standard wording – can be held on disk and printed out with any final additions without delay.

### 4. Make sure the invoice is correct
A mistake in an invoice provides the customer with a first-class excuse not to pay. The chances are that if a customer spots an error he will put the invoice to one side and wait for you to chase him for the money. When, after some time, you ring him up to ask for payment he will then simply refer to the mistake and you are back to square one.

Have a checklist of items which should appear in your invoice – to avoid errors of omission – and key points to check before mailing. Some of the basic essentials are:

● Any customer order number or reference.
● Description of the goods or service.
● Quantity, price extension and any tax.
● VAT registration number.
● Invoice date.
● Name of any particular individual or department to which the invoice should be sent.

The last item can be of considerable importance. If the invoice is merely addressed to the company it could spend a long time being passed around before it reaches a person who can do anything about it. The bigger the company, the longer the potential delay.

The key points to check might include:

● The accuracy of any calculations.
● The use of the correct invoicing address – this may not be the same as the delivery address.
● Whether or not any pre-payments have been allowed for.

Once again, a word processor can be helpful in that standard items such as the correct invoicing address can be stored on disk and need not be remembered each time.

### 5. Be sure that someone is responsible – and capable
Too often invoicing is left to be done when someone has the time

or is a job given to an inexperienced junior. Ideally there will be one individual responsible for checking references and credit-worthiness in the first place, keeping the sales ledger, preparing the invoices, maintaining a list of outstanding debts and chasing them up.

The best results are achieved if this person is a member of the management team and works closely with the sales department.

### 6. Maintain an aged debtors list

An up-to-date list showing you who owes you what and for how long is another basic essential. Unless the number of transactions is very small it is only too easy to overlook the unpaid invoice and for the weeks to skip by.

If you have a computer and use an accounting package an aged debtors list will almost certainly be part of the system. If so, use it. If not, a manual list will be required.

## Pursuing overdue payments

Despite all your best efforts there will be some overdue items, and these must also be dealt with methodically and with a professional touch.

To be successful, chasing up the customer whose payments are overdue requires rather more in the way of technique than simply writing a series of letters, each a bit tougher than the last.

Quite a lot of careful thought and preparation is required if time is not to be wasted and further delay in payment to be avoided. Consideration is needed, for example, of the particular customer you wish to chase and what you know about him. From your knowledge of how they operate and the character of the individuals you deal with you must decide the right time to make contact and how.

Will a telephone call be the most effective method and, if so, to whom?

Is a letter likely to produce results? Who should the letter be addressed to and what should it say?

Alternatively a personal call on the customer may be your best bet.

Whatever method you choose, some basic preparation is necessary.

## Preparation

- *The details*
  It is essential to have available the details of the debt you are dealing with. The larger the debtor company the more essential it is that you can quote chapter and verse all the relevant facts. Without this you are likely to make little progress.

- *Who are you talking to?*
  The person at the other end of the telephone line could be a difficult and unhelpful character. It is more likely that he or she:

  - is busy;
  - deals with dozens of suppliers;
  - has hundreds of payments to handle;
  - works to a rigid system;

  and pays more attention to people he thinks are helpful, i.e. can quote the facts that *he* wants.

  The golden rule is, 'Put yourself in the other person's shoes.' Look at the problem from his point of view and work out what will make it easier for him to meet your wishes.

- *What should you have ready?*
  The following checklist gives the information which will ease the way:

  - the customer's order number and date;
  - the product or service provided;
  - the date and place of supply;
  - despatch note and goods received note references;
  - your invoice number and date and to whom it was addressed.

  Not only will this type of information help the other person, it can remove obstacles set up by the person who is deliberately trying to delay or even avoid payment.

- *Sending a letter or making a visit*
  The information listed above is also needed if a letter is sent to the debtor or a personal call made. In these situations, providing the customer with a photocopy of your invoice can speed the process of sorting out the problem.

## Other aspects of presentation

- *Target the individual*
  A key factor in getting the money you are owed is contacting someone who can do something about your query. It is unlikely that the Chairman would be involved at this level, or that the office boy would have the authority.

- *Use the right tone*
  Very few people respond in a co-operative way to aggressive challenges – and even then only reluctantly. A hangover from the 1930s is the series of letters using Dickensian language and becoming ever more unpleasant. These, especially if pre-printed or obviously photocopies, are not the way to get the best result.
  Letters should be firm but friendly and avoid expressions such as:

  'It has come to our notice that . . .'

  '. . . your esteemed order of the 15th July . . .'

  '. . . regrettably must notify your goodselves . . .'

  '. . . must place the matter in the hands of our legal advisers . . .'

  '. . . we therefore respectfully request that you revert without further passage of time . . .'

  '. . . Consequent upon such delay we will have no alternative . . .'

  This sort of junk sounds as though it is produced by an accounting machine equipped with a dictionary of antique expressions. The person we are writing to (or telephoning) is a human being. We are human too so let's make the letter sound human.
  For example, 'Dear Mr Jones' sounds more human that 'Dear Sirs' (which sounds even more silly when the recipient is a woman).

- *Be human on the the telephone*
  The temptation to use the pompous style is normally less when using the telephone than in a letter. However, telephone users are not inhibited from aggressive and threatening statements – perhaps for some reason the medium encourages them. A constructive and friendly approach is likely to be more profitable.

- *Use ordinary, everyday language*
  Avoid expressions such as '... it has come to my notice ...'
  or '... your remittance is not yet to hand ...'

- *Set the tone with a few friendly words*
  It is not a waste of time or out of place in a business
  conversation. The time it takes to exchange a few civilities will
  be well rewarded if it establishes your relationship as a cordial
  one − or at worst, not a hostile one.

- *Avoid aggression*
  Don't accuse the individual or the company of being late with
  a payment or in any way of unfair dealing.

- *Ask for help*
  Almost everyone responds well to a request for help and most
  are even flattered by it.
     For example: 'I have a problem, Mrs Jones and need your
  help ...'
     You can then go on to explain that you have an invoice for
  which you have not been paid and if Mrs Jones can get the
  wheels moving you will be grateful.

## Working for agreement

Remember that you should be working to an agreement about how
and when you will be paid. You may have to make a concession or
two − especially if there is a problem. This might be an agreement
to delay payment of one invoice until a query is cleared up in
exchange for payment of another invoice by return. Quite
frequently a small concession can be of considerable value to the
customer and can remove the obstacle.

## The personal call

A personal call need not be the culmination of a series of fruitless
letters and telephone calls − with the intention of getting tough
with the customer. Personal calls can serve this purpose but are
also a good *alternative* to letters and the telephone.
  This is especially the case where a salesperson is calling on a
routine visit when, if briefed by the person responsible for

invoicing and receipts, he or she can raise the matter of overdue items. This, if done as part of a normal servicing visit, is less likely to appear threatening.

## Getting tough

If all your efforts are in vain you may end up without your money and needing to use more muscle. Legal action, which must be taken by or with the help of a competent lawyer, is taken as the last resort – and only when you are prepared to lose the customer for ever. However, customers who do not pay are bad customers and *should* be lost for ever.

You must form an opinion as to the cause for non-payment and act accordingly. Forcing the customer into bankruptcy will probably mean you will get nowhere and legal action would be a pointless waste of money. However, a lawyer's advice is worth taking.

Should there be a genuine dispute, e.g. about the amount owed, this may have to be resolved in the courts or by arbitration and, in this case also a lawyer's advice is essential.

Hopefully, tough action will not be necessary if you use good credit management and your office procedures are sound. Getting these things right in the first place can save you a lot of money. They might even save your business from going under.

### SUMMARY OF KEY POINTS

1. Money owed to you by your customers is costing you dearly – either by virtue of interest rates you are paying or by virtue of the investment earnings you are losing.

2. Prevention is cheaper than cure – and easier.

   ● Check out new customers for credit-worthiness and reputation.
   ● Formally agree terms of payment – and if at all possible get money up front or in stage payments.
   ● Make sure you have a sound system for preparing accurate invoices promptly and mailing them without delay.

● Make someone specifically responsible for invoicing – trained and capable.
● Monitor outstanding debts. Use an aged-debtors list.

3. Chase debts intelligently using a constructive and friendly approach backed up by preparation and attention to detail. Be human and use human language when chasing debts.

4. If you have to get tough, consult a lawyer before using the courts.

# CHAPTER 4

# *REDUCING ADMINISTRATION COSTS*

Administration costs such as stationery purchases, office cleaning, insurances and postage tend to be overlooked in many businesses. No one challenges the cost of printing the business cards or the latest price list. No one thinks twice about the rental cost of the photocopier, and even if there is some grumbling when someone insists on buying more filing cabinets, little attention is given to the possibilities of a cheaper alternative course of action. Such areas as these are susceptible to fairly quick cost saving. With a little effort, *some* worthwhile results should emerge after about a month.

## Why are administration costs overlooked?

It is often claimed that administration costs are so small compared with, say, office rents and salaries that any savings will have an insignificant effect on the company profits. This can be a big mistake and time spent on them can have a worthwhile pay-off.

Take for example the typical financial situation in a service business, say a company of graphic designers. The single largest cost is likely to be the salaries of the employees. The next largest item of expense will probably be the rent of a building used for offices and studios. The remainder will be taken up with office supplies, telephone bills, accounting fees and the like.

The breakdown of the expenditure of income will be roughly as follows:

| | |
|---|---|
| Salaries | 60% |
| Building | 25% |
| Other | 10% |
| | 95% |

The remaining 5% will be pre-tax profit.

It is not unnatural for someone to say that since 85% (or whatever) of the cost is for practical purposes irreducible there is not much point in a cost saving exercise. They might add that only 10% of income is a potential field for expenditure reduction and any results will be marginal. The fact is that if the 10% can be reduced to 9% then pre-tax profits will be increased by 20%! To achieve such an increase in profits by finding more customers and producing more work could be extremely difficult and in some cases not even possible. A good hard look at all the 'bits and pieces' of expenditure is always a good idea.

What then should be looked at and what can be done? Let's start with some of the bigger items.

## Company location

Perhaps the most promising administration cost saving action a business can take is to relocate to premises in a less expensive area. Yes, there are many difficulties to overcome – not least the prospect of losing valuable staff who will not or cannot move and are unable to travel to and from the new location. However the profit incentive can be substantial. A company moving from a large city to a provincial town can cut space costs by as much as 75%. It is also likely that facilities such as car parking spaces will be more available and labour costs less.

There will of course be some one-off costs to be taken into account, including legal fees, compensation to staff, removal charges, telephone and other installations, and reprinting stationery. All such outlay can be amply recouped within the first year.

## Insurance

This is a subject which too few business people really understand and which far too many leave to a broker. Although an insurance broker is the agent of his client and acts on his behalf, his fee comes not from his client but from the insurer. The fee is often simply a percentage added to the premium and agreed between the broker and the insurer. Notwithstanding any rules and regulations which demand that the broker must offer the best advice, there is often a potential conflict of interests.

A broker may suggest placing business with the insurer who is willing to pay him the most commission – even if the cover is not the best available to meet his client's needs. In addition he may recommend a breadth of cover which is not necessary. More cover means higher premiums (which you pay) and higher commission (which the broker gets).

## The first requirement

Start by deciding what insurance you *really* need. Some (e.g. employer's liability) will be a legal requirement. Others (e.g. fire) may be highly desirable. There may be some, such as product liability or errors and omissions, which you can live without – providing you are well aware of the risk you are taking.

Consideration should be given to your present position and some questions asked:

● How probable is it that a claim is really likely to be made?
● Have we ever made any claims?
● How vulnerable are we?

One small business with fairly substantial insurance cover on its premises discovered that the landlord also insured the premises. The not inconsiderable premiums paid had been unnecessary and, if a claim had been made, it is likely that both insurers would have resisted it on the basis that double insurance had been involved. This provision is likely to appear in the small print of your policy suitably shrouded in insurance jargon.

Let us suppose that, having looked carefully at all your policies, you have decided that some (or all) of them are essential. The next potential area for saving is the size of the deductible and the size of the limit.

## The deductible

Also known as an excess, the deductible is the amount that you will 'retain' in the event of a loss. If, say, your deductible for storm damage is £1000 and the insurers agree that a loss is valued at £5000, then you will receive only £4000. The first £1000 of the loss will be borne by you.

Naturally, the lower the deductible the higher the premium. Many deductibles are set at zero which means a maximum premium when in fact a small retention (a jargon term meaning deductible) will result in something much lower. Brokers tend to propose zero deductibles as this increases their earnings. Alternatively, the fact that a deductible is an available option may not be pointed out at all.

Find out what the premium will be for various levels of deductible and decide which suits you best. You may be quite willing to pay the first few hundred or so of any loss which might arise in exchange for a lower premium. Only you can decide, in the light of what your business can stand and the probability of a loss arising. If any loss of any size could put you out of business then you will need a zero deductible – not a common situation.

## The limit

The limit is the maximum amount of money that the insurer will pay you regardless of the size of the loss. If a fire damages your warehouse to the tune of £1,000,000 and your limit is £500,000 then the smaller figure is all you will get.

There is a tendency to opt for limits which are too high – and thereby to pay a higher premium. This course of action is often taken in the interest of 'safety' when in fact it is wholly unnecessary. Thought should be given to the worst possible loss scenario. After careful consideration, you could find that you can live with a lower limit and benefit from a reduced premium.

## Shop around

Another potentially profitable step is to offer your business to two or more brokers and/or to go direct to the insurance companies yourself. Brokers react to the threat of competition in the same way that everyone else does. Simply leaving everything to the same broker year after year can mean that he will settle into a comfortable routine of renewing 'as before'. This reduces the broker's work to a minimum but could mean you are paying too much for the cover you get.

## Bank charges

This is another area where too much can be paid for want of a little effort.

Your bank manager will slap a charge on you for every transaction – mainly payments into and out of your account. These charges are negotiable whatever your bank manager may say. It can pay handsomely to knock a penny or two off each transaction charge, especially if your business involves a multitude of small payments.

One small business dealing in low value items was paying in around 1200 cheques per month. The charge for each cheque was 20p resulting in a cost of about £240 per month.

Negotiation resulted in a reduction of 5p per cheque and an annual saving of £720 p.a. Not a king's ransom, you may say, but equivalent to quite a lot of sales effort.

### The 'My hands are tied' ploy

If the bank manager tells you that he is unable to negotiate because charge rates are set by 'head office', tell him you will shop around for another bank (or even another branch of the same one); he is likely to find a way to persuade 'head office' to be more flexible. If this approach fails, then open an account at a building society and pay all your cheques into it. At monthly intervals, or when otherwise required, a lump sum can be withdrawn from the building society and paid into your bank. This will save you all but one transaction charge and you will gain some interest from the building society in the meantime.

## Heating and lighting

These are costs which seem to be subject to an inevitable annual increase as the producers of electricity and other fuels announce their routine price rises.

Small to medium consumers are often the worst hit as they are less likely to be able to negotiate special rates which are enjoyed by major users of power. However, a renegotiation is worth a try and this should be the first action taken.

### Try some cost prevention

Measures of a preventive nature can be taken, such as:

● Investing in insulation and eliminating draughts. The cost of installing efficient insulation is normally recovered in the form of savings in a relatively short time.

● A thermostatically controlled central heating system is likely to repay its costs if it replaces a miscellaneous collection of hot air blowers and electric heaters.

If you already have a central heating system ensure that it is up-to-date – especially the control system. The thermostat may be inefficient, and replacing it with a modern microchip-based control system could save a lot of money in quite a short time.

● Installing a modern lighting system – particularly if this means replacing the traditional light bulb with strip lighting or modern bulbs which (a) last longer and (b) give greater light for less power.

● Check that heating (and hot water) levels are not set unnecessarily high. A temperature reduction of one or two degrees cuts down heat loss and saves more than you might think. A hot water tank loses heat from radiation at a rate which is the square of the difference between tank temperature and ambient temperature. Dropping the temperature by a degree or two cuts the heat loss significantly.

● Install time switches or daylight reaction switches to ensure that lights will be turned off when no longer required even if employees forget them.

## Space utilisation

Money can only be saved on space either if space can be made available for sub-letting or if taking on *more* space can be delayed. Both options are good money savers and should be followed up vigorously. There is a tendency to accept the way in which space is used because we are used to it. When the space is full there is a knee-jerk reaction to find more space rather than making more efficient use of what we already have.

The following action should be taken:

● Clear out all junk. Much too much paper tends to be stored in offices, and all kinds of junk in factories and workshops.

Ask the questions:

'Do we really need it?'

'When did we last use it?'
'Can we sell it?'

Among the items which are often unnecessarily kept are old computer listings, materials left over from a long-completed job, machine tools no longer used and spare parts – sometimes obsolescent ones.

A small company in the suburbs of London conducted a clearing-out exercise having found that more space – apparently necessary – would increase rent costs by about 30%. The clear-out removed the need to take on more space and a welcome couple of thousand pounds was gained as a result of selling metal to a scrap dealer.

● Use 'vertical' space. The space above shoulder height in both workshops and offices is often unused. In an office it is common to find the traditional drawer-type filing cabinets, which take up a lot of low-level space. The area taken up is much more than just the square footage of floor on which they stand: it is necessary to have a free space in front of each cabinet to allow someone to stand in order to open the drawers – in addition to two or three feet required for the open drawer itself. The 'drawer opening' space can be saved by using lateral filing racks. These take up the width of the files and standing area only *and* can use more of the vertical space. They also have the advantage that the files are visible and thus easier to find.

● *Plan* the use of space as opposed to allowing things just to happen. Busy factory floors are often cluttered with bins, rubbish tubs and bits and pieces which people move from place to place more or less at random. There is normally a 'best place' for each item which should be marked with lines painted on the floor. Some discipline in returning things to the designated position not only makes better use of the space available but also means that employees waste less time in finding things. Aim to reduce the number of times that someone says 'Who the hell put that there? I've been searching for it for half an hour.'

## Water charges

Perhaps you can obtain a better deal with the water supply company. One way is to have a meter installed. The installation will probably have to be at your expense but it could save you a lot of money if you are not a heavy user. A London firm of design and water industry consultants claim that they have saved up to 90% of the water charges for clients in the London area.

Even if a metered system is not desirable – or you already have one – check your tariff. You could find that substantial savings could be made by switching tariffs. This is not something the water supply company is likely to tell you about, so ask them.

## Photocopying

It is amazing how businesses coped before photocopiers were invented. It is also amazing how much can be spent in a year on photocopying. Not infrequently the cost is unnecessarily high.

The first thing to consider is what type of photocopier you need. That is to say, *really* need.

### The two main types of copier

Broadly speaking, photocopiers fall into two types, high-speed machines and low-speed machines. The high-speed photocopiers tend to be larger, cost more to rent or buy, and are designed for mass copying.

The high speed is a definite advantage if you need to turn out hundreds of copies of, say, price lists or circulars. They are also necessary if you are frequently copying large originals such as very lengthy reports or manuscripts and speed is important.

If, however, the great bulk of your photocopying involves one or two copies of an original, then it is likely that a slow-speed machine will be less costly. It should be borne in mind that in many if not most offices the average 'run length' is about 1.5 per original. Most of these runs will involve a single-page original.

### Check – keep a record

It is useful to keep a record for two or three weeks of the work done on the photocopier to see how many originals were involved and how many copies were taken during each run. This will give you a much more reliable figure to go on than the 'guesstimates' that staff will come up with. Memories tend to be dominated by the occasional, even rare, very long run and the fact that most work is in single copies is overlooked.

## Cost per copy

The records will also enable you to see how much you are paying per copy. This is the real crunch in controlling photocopier costs.

Let us suppose for example that you are renting a fairly fast machine for £50 per month. At varying levels of use your cost per copy will work out as follows:

| Monthly rent | No. of copies | Copy cost (pence) |
|---|---|---|
| £ | | |
| 50 | 100 | 50 |
| 50 | 200 | 25 |
| 50 | 500 | 10 |
| 50 | 1000 | 5 |
| 50 | 2000 | 2.5 |

Suppose that you find that you are taking around 1000 copies per month with a cost per copy of 5p. A slower machine at a rental of, say, £30 per month yielding a copy cost of 3p will be cheaper *and* will also be cheaper than the other alternative of using a high street copy shop charging, say, 4p per copy. The importance of working out the cost per copy for the alternative types of machine, or an outside service, is obvious.

## Check the 'extras'

Also important is to look at the extras which you may be paying for and not really need. Facilities such as colour copying, choice of colour (normally black or blue copies), double-side copying, magnification and reduction are all nice to have but will cost you more. The true need for such features should be coldly assessed before rushing into something which will be nice to have but of little real value.

## How are you paying

Another aspect of photocopy costs which needs careful thought is the way in which the machine and associated costs are paid for. In years gone by almost all machines were offered on modest rental terms with a metered charge for the copies taken.

It is still possible to find manufacturers offering this system, but there are many others including:

- Monthly rental charges which are fairly modest but, and this needs watching, a hefty monthly 'maintenance' charge.
- Interest-free hire purchase terms.
- Deferred payment terms.
- Fixed term rental.

Some care is needed in sorting out which scheme suits you best and is most economic. The approach, having taken into account tax implications, is always to work back to the cost per copy based on your expected level of use of the machine.

## Don't forget supplies costs

Remember to take into account the cost of any supplies – especially those which you may be contracted to buy from the supplier of the machine.

# Communications

This is an area where rapid technological changes are moving the cost goalposts.

Probably the most significant developments in recent years are the facsimile machine and computer-to-computer links, with the latter taking the lead in bringing about changes.

However, computers, fax and telex all have one thing in common. They all operate on the telephone line or other links provided by the common carriers such as British Telecom, Mercury and Bell.

This simplifies the choice of method when seeking economies, to comparing the speed with which the equipment can pass the message down the telephone wire. The slower the speed the higher the cost, since the line will be in use for longer.

Generally computers are faster than fax and fax is faster than telex. However, the time taken is not necessarily determined by the 'line speed' i.e. the theoretical speed at which the machine plus line can transmit data. The speed with which the operator can depress keys on the keyboard may be the dominating factor. Telex can work at speeds of around 15 characters per second. This sounds terrific until we realise that operators cannot work at that speed. The same consideration may apply when using computer-to-computer links. The computer's ability to shovel thousands of characters a second down the line may be negated if the system is operator dependent.

## Prepare data off-line

Savings can be made by ensuring that data is prepared 'off-line' by, for instance, putting telex messages on a word-processor disk and transmitting direct from the disk. It may take as much time for the word processor operator to compose the telex as it would take the telex operator to depress the telex keys, but the telephone line is not in use at the same time. This cuts your telephone bills.

The cost calculation to be made in working out what method to use in communicating is the number of characters or words per minute which can be transmitted. There will, of course, be other considerations such as the nature of the data to be transmitted. Fax is ideal for drawings, sketches, formulae and prepared documents. Telex may be more appropriate for short, simple messages and may be the only available method when communicating with parts of the world where fax is not yet in common use.

## Controlling telephone costs

The telephone, used in its traditional way for voice traffic, can be an expensive item in the administration costs budget. The facility is much taken for granted, with a tendency to adopt the same attitude to the resulting bills. Picking up the phone can be almost a reflex action in a variety of situations. A little thought can result in some savings. Managers and employees should be taught to think before making a call and to ask themselves the following questions:

- Is my call really necessary?
- Will anything be gained by making the call?
- Would a pre-printed letter or card be cheaper and as effective?
- Can I make the call during an off-peak charge period?
- Have I prepared for the call, i.e. thought about what I am

going to say, assembled my facts and generally taken steps to prevent the call being unnecessarily prolonged?

The last point draws attention to aspects of telephone technique in which all phone users should be trained. Actions which can increase the cost of a call include:

- Hanging on for someone who is not immediately available.
- Failing to have in mind an alternative individual or extension if the first person asked for is not available.
- Spending too much time in social chit-chat.

Social chatter can be a problem when the person at the other end wants to prolong it – at your expense. Most people are inhibited from interrupting as this may seem discourteous or offensive. This need not be the case if the right technique is used.

Simply breaking in on the other person's excited flow may well sound rude – unless the interruption is prefaced by the other person's name. Think about it. If you hear your name whilst in mid-flow you will stop. What is more, you will not think the interruption is rude.

Two useful techniques for saving time are:

1. Interrupt, *using the person's name* and then ask a question. This will enable you to bring the conversation back to the subject you wish to discuss without causing offence.

2. Use the person's name and then make an excuse to end the conversation, for example: 'George, sorry, but I will have to go. I have a visitor just arrived outside my door ...'

## Should Big Brother be watching?

Manufacturers of call logging systems claim big savings as a result of installing their equipment. Call logging involves attaching an electronic device to the switchboard so that every time a call is made a record is kept. The record, which can be printed out whenever required, will list the calls made from each extension and show the time and duration of the call, the number dialled and the cost. The system undoubtedly has a sobering effect on the more enthusiastic phone users and does inhibit unauthorised use.

The system is particularly valuable in organisations employing a lot of office workers such as large accounting or law practices, insurance brokers, travel agents.

> In one case a company employing about 100 office staff discovered that regular calls were being made at about 7 p.m. to a foreign number. These calls were lengthy, expensive and could not be explained. Investigation revealed that a cleaner, employed in the evenings, was using the firm's telephone to call his relatives overseas.

Such unauthorised use can be very expensive – one company reckoned that about 10% of its telephone bill was accounted for by personal calls.

## Can the Post Office help?

In some businesses postage costs can be a significant item of expense. If you are a major mail user – perhaps sending out regular price lists, leaflets, brochures and mail shots you may qualify for a discount from the Post Office.

This discount can be substantial where volumes are very high, but you may be required to carry out some pre-sorting into postal areas. The pre-sorting, if properly organised, should not present a problem and additional discounts may be available if all your mail is postcoded and again if mail is ready for collection at a time stipulated by the post office.

These are only some of the possibilities open to you and a discussion with your nearest main post office can put you in the picture.

## Does it pay to be second class?

Some countries have a first and second class mail system, and if you are trading in one of them you must ask how much of your mail is sent first class. Probably all of it. If so, thought should be given to the necessity of paying extra to gain a day or two in delivery.

Suppose, for example, that you are intending to mail 5000 letters advising potential customers of your latest offering. Suppose also that you want them to know about it on or about 1 September to give them time to order for the Christmas trade.

If you have the letters ready for mailing on, say, 28 August then they will meet your deadline at the second class rate. There is no point in delaying posting until 31 August and then paying additional postage for the privilege. Would it, in any case, matter if the customer received his letters on 2 September as opposed to 1 September? Would you be less likely to get the business?

A realistic attitude can save you money.

## Are you underweight?

Surveys have shown that many, if not most, mailings are well below the weight allowed for the minimum price. This means that businesses can be losing opportunities to include a price list or other information with, say, routine correspondence. It will cost no more and, although not always easy to organise, is another way to make a saving.

## Is the courier really necessary?

Motor-cycle (and pedal-cycle) courier services have multiplied enormously in recent years. Leather-clad young men and women are a common sight in the larger towns and cities, weaving their way through the traffic.

The charge for these services is not normally unreasonable but is very high when compared with postal costs.

Probably the single most useful feature of courier services is speed. A customer rings up and asks for a drawing or a sample or whatever which he needs today. The courier is often the only means of delivery other than sending one of your own employees in a taxi. However, analysis of the reasons for using couriers in the past is likely to show that by no means all are based on unavoidable external demands made upon you.

## The cost of failing to plan

Examination of the use of couriers in a medium-sized British company revealed that about 50% of the despatches were the result of lack of planning – or even negligence.

Work being carried out to a deadline was often allowed to slip behind schedule, resulting in a last-minute panic and the extra expense of employing a courier to save the day. In a few cases a courier was employed where entirely unnecessary as the deadline could have been met in a cheaper way and there was plenty of time to do so. If you are not careful couriers can become an expensive habit and only too often a longstop which should never be used: 'Don't worry about it — if we leave it until next week we can always use a courier.'

## General supplies and services

There is a considerable range of supplies and services which cost money but tend to receive insufficient attention. Many items are individually small in their contribution to administrative costs and because of this are too infrequently scrutinised.

The list can include such things as:

> Printing
> Typewriter and word processor maintenance
> Soap and other toilet supplies
> Cleaning — offices, windows, carpets, etc.
> Laundry
> Payroll preparation
> Security
> Vending machine supplies
> Catering
> Office plants.

In addition there will be 'one-offs' from time to time such as redecoration of offices and lavatories.

The first question to be asked in respect to a product or service we are buying is 'Do we need it at all?' The answer will often be 'yes' but sometimes it is 'no', in which case a saving can be promptly made. If the item is unavoidable the next questions to answer are:

● *Can we negotiate a lower price?*
This can be done more frequently than one might imagine. The converse is passively to accept the supplier's annual 'inflation increase' — something which may not be necessary at all.

● *Is there an alternative supplier who will give us a better deal?*

● *Is there a cheaper substitute product?* An example might be paper towels instead of roller towels or vice versa.

● *Can we do it in-house?*

The possibility of doing for yourselves what you pay someone else to do deserves serious consideration.

Examples from real life include the company which gave its small laundry contract to the wife of an employee and the company whose own employees redecorated the offices over weekends. In both cases the cost was lower and the employees were glad of the extra income.

A similar approach can be made to catering or office plants and in one case typewriter maintenance was done by an employee and her husband.

A substantial attack on the costs of general supplies and services can save you money – as was found by a service company employing about 200 office workers. Everything from lavatory paper to telephone lines was looked at. The saving was about £10,000 a year.

## Is there anything you can share?

There are many businesses housed in the same premises as other businesses and many who live side-by-side in business parks (the posh new name for trading estates). This proximity offers an opportunity to reduce administration costs, among others, which few seem to take advantage of.

The opportunity lies in the fact that, providing a sensible arrangement can be worked out, two or more businesses can share a facility and thus substantially reduce the fixed and operating costs.

### Cutting printing costs

A real-life example was the sharing of in-house printing facilities by two companies in the same building. They shared the cost of buying an offset litho machine and training an operator. The company which housed the machine paid the salary of the operator and purchased the paper, ink and other materials. Work done for the other company was then billed to them on an at-cost basis. This arrangement avoided the need to purchase two machines – which if used individually would have been under-utilised. The sharing also increased the size of orders for paper, plates, etc., enabling both companies to enjoy the benefits of bulk purchase discounts. There was also a salary saving by virtue of having only one operator rather than two.

## What are the possibilities for sharing?

Depending on the nature of your business and where you are situated, possibilities for sharing could include some of the following:

Photocopying
Mail room
Messenger service
Security
Word processing
Cleaning
Invoicing and debt chasing
Payroll preparation
Building maintenance
Switchboard.

The obstacle to sharing is often an obsession with confidentiality. Managers may be afraid that the other company will acquire 'secret' information – particularly if something like invoicing is involved. This is a much exaggerated problem which tends to disappear if the whole question is viewed objectively. In any case the work involved can be organised to limit the amount of information available to the company not entitled to it. Working out the cash savings can also put the confidentiality problem into perspective!

It is important to work out in advance exactly how the sharing will be done and who pays for what. Agreements must be reached in dealing with any conflicting priorities and the supervision of work. These aspects sometimes present real difficulties, but they can be overcome with the application of some commonsense and goodwill. Again, the cash advantages provide a spur to finding ways round any obstacles.

## What about the perks?

If your sales representative has a company car and uses it every day to visit customers, that is not a perk.

72

If, on the other hand, two or three directors each have a company car for status reasons then those cars are perks. The cost of providing them can be reduced either by postponing replacement or by replacing them with less expensive models.

Other methods for cutting perk costs which have worked in practice include:

- Limiting all flights less than 4 hours in duration to economy tickets.
- Using club or business class for flights of from 4−6 hours − and allowing first class travel only for journeys over 6 hours.
- Applying travel class rates according to distance or time and not seniority.
- Generally cutting back on in-house entertaining; offering wine only − no spirits.

Naturally there will be some wailing and gnashing of teeth and this must be taken into account. However, since most perks go to the more senior people, their reduction should be understood and accepted.


## Making it all happen − a reminder

In Chapter 2 the point was made that to improve your chances of achieving some real results the various jobs to be done should be allocated to specified people. In addition a deadline date is necessary in order to prevent the exercise drifting on from month to month.

The same applies when examining administration costs. Each area to be examined should be made the responsibility of an individual, with a deadline date laid down for completing the work and reporting the results. Taking such a positive line could give you the same reward as that gained by a company which cut £140,000 off its annual office administration bill. This was worth over a million pounds in sales.


### SUMMARY OF KEY POINTS

1. Challenging the need for 'minor' purchases and the cost is as necessary as it is for major items. A small saving can represent a significant percentage increase on profit.

2. Be sure that you buy the insurance that you really need — with sensible levels of deductible and limit.

3. Don't take your bank charges lying down. Negotiate for a better deal.

4. Check your heating and lighting costs. Look into the likely savings which more modern controls and equipment can bring you.

5. Consider whether you should be located in a cheaper area. It will cost you money to move, but you could make a substantial saving in time.

6. Space is expensive. Don't waste money storing junk, use vertical space and *plan* space utilisation.

7. Check your water supply tariff — and whether or not you should be metered.

8. Work out which photocopying system will give you the lowest cost per copy. Avoid paying for unnecessary facilities.

9. What is the cheapest way to transmit the types of messages required by your business!
   Compare the line costs — based on transmission time — of the options open to you.
   Train your people in economic use of the telephone. Consider time-logging as a means to cut heavy telephone bills.

10. Discuss your postal needs with the post office. You may be able to arrange cheaper rates for bulk mailing.
   Be realistic about using 1st class post and make full use of the weight allowance that you pay for.

11. Check over the prices of all your general supplies and services. Do you need them? Can you buy something more cheaply? Is there a service you can do better for yourself?

12. Look for opportunities to share a facility and share the cost.

13. Think about perks. Can these be cut back without causing a revolution?

14. Don't forget – if you want something to happen – allocate responsibilities and set a deadline.

# CHAPTER 5

# *REDUCING THE COST OF PAPERWORK*

All paperwork – forms, record cards, computer listings and the like – should carry a business health warning.

While good paperwork can help to cut costs and improve profits, the other kind can be seriously damaging. So, too, can the absence of a desirable form or record.

This means that a good look at paper used in the business should be made and a lot of questions asked and answered (honestly).

## What should paperwork do for us?

Essentially, the purposes of forms and other documents fall into one or more of the following categories:

- To record information.
- To communicate information.
- To act as a tool for calculation and decision-taking.

Even the back of an old envelope (which is likely to be a 'bad' piece of paperwork) can be used for all these purposes. For example, a foreman might jot down some production figures (recording) and send the envelope to the production manager (communicating). The production manager might then work out some costs and decide to change production plans (calculating and making a decision).

## What bad paperwork does

Bad paperwork will fail to do one or more of these functions

| Name: | Department: | Date: | |
|---|---|---|---|
| Type of vehicle: | Registration no.: | Repairs this month: | Cost of repairs: |

| | | |
|---|---|---|
| Mileage at first of month | | Remarks |
| Mileage at end of month | | |
| Mileage covered | | |
| Petrol purchased (gallons) | | |
| Cost per gallon | | |
| Total cost | * | |
| Cost per mile | | |
| Oil purchased (pints) | | |
| Cost per pint | | |
| Total cost | * | |
| Cost per mile | | |
| Cost of petrol | | |
| Cost of oil | | |
| Total cost | | |
| | | |
| Private mileage | | |
| Cost per mile | | |
| Total cost | | |

* Attach receipts

| Signed: | Dept.: | Date: |
|---|---|---|

Figure 5. A badly designed form which lost money.

properly or at all. The result will be that we can end up with:

- Partial information.
- Wrong information.
- Misleading information.
- Valueless information.

We can also, if we get the paperwork wrong, fail to communicate in time, to the right people, or at all. Calculation and decision-taking can be misdirected or invalidated by bad paperwork.

Figure 5, on page 77, is a real-life example of the sort of thing that can happen if we fail to pay enough attention to what we are doing with, in this case, forms.

The purpose of the form illustrated – designed by a man now dead who worked for a company now extinct – was to keep track of expenditure on company cars and to ensure that private mileage expense was reclaimed from car users.

Let us look at the logic of the form:

1. The top horizontal line has a blank space at the right-hand end for no apparent reason.

2. The space for repairs on the second line is too small for anything but the briefest description; and the cost of repairs is in any case ignored in the calculation which follows.

3. The 'mileage covered' entry is straightforward enough except that it would be much easier to subtract the start of the month figure from the end of the month figure if the former were placed under the latter to avoid an 'upside down' subtraction.

4. The number of gallons of petrol purchased seems to be irrelevant and takes no account of how much was in the tank at the start of the month and the end of the month.

5. The cost per gallon allows for only one answer when in fact petrol prices vary from one place to another. Some car users worked out an average which was particularly misleading as, in some cases, it was not weighted by the number of gallons at each price.

6. The total cost should have been the sum of the value of all petrol purchased. Due to the use of only one price per gallon (sometimes shown as a misleading average) multiplied by the number of gallons, the total recorded was frequently wrong.

7.  A similar result was achieved with oil costs.

8.  Cost per mile is now required for the second time but in respect of oil only. (Cost of repairs, likely to be much larger and in fact meant to include servicing and replacements, is still required.)

9.  The cost of petrol and oil are again recorded and a total cost demanded for the third time.

10. The private mileage cost per mile is asked for, but without a means to work it out.

11. The block devoted to 'Remarks' on the right of the form suggests that the designer did not know what to do with this space.

12. At the bottom the user's department is required and the date. Both of these items are also included in the top line of the form.

All in all, this form resulted in much confusion and waste of costly time. The designer had only a vague idea of what he wanted and put little thought into the design. Thankfully, not all forms are as bad as this 'classic', but many forms include one or two of the errors described.

## What is your paperwork like?

A thorough review of every form, 'little black books', index cards and everything else can save you a lot of money. In addition you can cut down on aggravation, delay, muddle and generally make the business more efficient.

### Is it necessary?

The first question to ask is, 'Do we really need it?' There should be a real purpose *and benefit* from every piece of paper in the system.

If there is any doubt as to the value of something, then it is a prime candidate for the scrap heap. Cutting out a form or whatever not only cuts out work (someone fills it in, someone possibly reads it and someone files it), but also saves printing costs.

Sometimes a document does have a real value, but the copies distributed to all and sundry are not necessary. It is common to find that Mr X thinks he should have a copy ('to keep me in touch') and Mr Y is on the circulation list because he thinks his status demands it. ('I like to keep an eye on things'). These copies can be dumped.

If a document appears to be borderline or the copies questionable, ask yourself the following questions:

- What useful action takes place as a result of someone receiving the paper?
- Is any useful action possible at all? The facts and figures could, for example, be too out of date when finally available to be used as a guide to future action.
- What would we lose if the document is scrapped?
- What would we gain if the document is scrapped?

## If essential, can it be improved?

Suppose that, say, the salesmen's call report form is essential and the monthly sales report really is helpful to planning and control; the next question to ask is, 'Can we simplify it?'

Many documents are designed badly (see Figure 5 again) or needs have changed since the document was first introduced. The chances are that there is redundant data which can be removed and/or the logic of the form can be improved.

There is often also a 'family' of documents which, if examined together, will offer opportunities for simplification or even elimination. There is a technique for analysing families of documents known as the X-Chart.

## How to use the X-Chart

The documents concerned are collected together and the contents entered into an analysis chart (see Figure 6 on page 81). Scrutiny of the way the contents of the documents are distributed will suggest ways to cut out work and duplication. For instance, the information given on the documents in Figure 6 shows that all the data given on document 4 also appears on document 1. It could well be possible to scrap document 4 altogether if users of it are given document 1 instead. They can ignore 'department' and other unwanted items.

Similarly, documents 2 and 3 could be merged into one to eliminate yet another piece of paper.

Of course, unless confidentiality of some of the data is paramount, the whole lot could be merged into one piece of paper to be used by everyone.

| Item | Document 1 | Document 2 | Document 3 | Document 4 |
|------|:---:|:---:|:---:|:---:|
| Name | X | X | X | X |
| Address | X | | | X |
| Joining date | X | X | X | |
| Department | X | | | |
| Salary grade | | X | | |
| N.I. number | | | X | |
| Payroll number | | | X | |
| Next of kin | X | | | X |
| | | | | |

Figure 6. Using an X-Chart.

## Computer listings

The X-Chart is especially valuable when looking at computer output. One of the most abused advantages of the computer is its ability to churn out stacks of information in a wide variety of ways – at high speed. It is only too easy for someone to demand and get a variation of a computer listing.

Suppose, for example, the company computer produces a listing like this:

DATE:                                    STOCK ITEM REPORT

DESC          CODE          GRADE          QTY HELD

Such a listing might be used by someone to check stock levels. Along comes someone else who is interested in usage rates of the items stored and he asks for a report showing:

DATE:                                    USAGE REPORT

DESC          CODE          GRADE          QTY USED

This demand will probably be met by some new software and an additional computer run.

In fact it is almost certain that the two reports can be combined, and only one computer run carried out to satisfy both needs.

The stock item report shows the quantity held in stock. This figure is probably arrived at by adding opening stock to additions to stock and then subtracting the quantity used. The latter amount is exactly what is asked for on the second report and is probably suppressed by the computer for printing purposes.

The combined report which, from one computer run only, satisfies both needs will look like this:

| DATE: | | STOCK USAGE & BALANCE REPORT | | |
|-------|------|-------|----------|----------|
| DESC | CODE | GRADE | QTY USED | QTY HELD |

Further investigation may well show that adding opening quantity and stock additions to the listing will be useful, if only to the accountants. The cost will be the same.

## Form design

The design of computer listings – in effect a type of form used to communicate information – leads to the whole question of document design. This is a much neglected subject. The importance of knowing how to design forms properly was illustrated by the example in Figure 5. Failure to get it right can result in wasted time, errors (and the cost of correcting them) and a multitude of foul-ups. The problem is that so many people consider themselves to be experts on form design when they have not had even the most elementary training in how to go about it.

One such was the man who designed an order form for use by salespeople and would-be customers.

The form omitted to allow for product code numbers and delivery address – as opposed to invoicing address. The resulting confusion was both costly and damaging to the company reputation until, after about a month, a properly designed form was introduced. What then are the basic essentials in form design?

## Some key points to watch

If you can see a clear advantage for having the form then its purpose must be clearly established. Then ask:

● Who will use the form?
● Where will it be used?
● How will it be used?

Clarifying these points will help to ensure that the design is right.

### Will the form be easily understood?

Ideally, all forms will be self-explanatory – or will be accompanied by a set of simple instructions for use of the form. However, in business we can hardly expect our customers to read accompanying instructions and if the form is for internal use we do not want our employees to spend time reading the instructions. The target must be to make the form itself tell the user what is wanted. Ways to do this include:

● A clear explanatory title.
● The use of unambiguous terms. If 'quantity' is to be entered for example, make it clear what this means. Does it mean the number of cartons or the number of items in the carton?

### How is the form to be filled in?

A form which is to be completed on a typewriter or word processor will need horizontal spacing to suit these machines, and ideally will be designed on the machine itself. If not, we will end up with that all too common problem of a typed line appearing on a dividing line. Worse still, the data can end up in the wrong box. The result can be disastrous.

### Where will the form be used?

A form to be filled in by a surveyor standing in a 30 mph wind on top of a building needs different consideration from one to be completed by a clerk in an office.

The weight and quality of paper needed should not be overlooked, both from the point of view of the environment

83

(including greasy work benches) and the means of recording the data. Ball-point pens need a fairly firm surface with some strength or backing, while pencils do not write well on glossy surfaces.

## Does the form save time or waste it?

The sequence of operations in completing the form and reading the entries should be logical. In addition, the spaces provided should be adjusted to suit the amount of data to be entered and not the length of the title.

Getting this wrong leads to:

● Entries being cramped and difficult to read.

or

● Entries being misinterpreted, being partially under the wrong heading.

Both of these cause mistakes and confusion and these in turn waste time and cost money.

## Pre-print wherever possible

Another common time-waster is a failure to pre-print standard information. For example, an order form could have all the products and their codes pre-printed. This saves the salesman or customer the time required to write them out *and* prevents the use of inadequate or incorrect codes and descriptions.

## Avoid repetition

Unnecessary repetition of information is yet another time-waster. In one real-life case the address of the person required to complete the form was asked for *three times*. If you present your customer with this kind of repetition he will be at best irritated and at worst form a poor view of your efficiency.

## Reducing the cost of manufacturing your forms

Printing is expensive and many businesses spend a considerable percentage of their expenditure budget on forms, brochures, record cards and the like. The following are features which *add to* cost and should be avoided if at all possible:

- More than one colour on each sheet.
- Perforations.
- Serial numbering.
- Names of recipients on sheets of a multi-part set.
- Holes (e.g. for ring binders).
- Binding and padding.
- Non-standard paper sizes.

It is important also to work out the most sensible quantity to order. The cost per copy goes down as print runs increase, but there is not likely to be a saving if the quantity ordered is likely to last for years. Losses will arise from deterioration and the forms could become obsolete before they are used up.

## Names can cause trouble

It is a common practice when designing forms with a number of copies (multi-part sets) to put on each copy the name of the person for whom it is intended. On the face of it this can help to prevent mis-routing and ensure that important information reaches the person who needs it. This is normally true − for a time.

The problem is that people retire or otherwise disappear from the scene with the result that there can be confusion and doubt as to where a copy should be sent. The problem can be avoided by marking copies with a job title such as 'Accountant' or 'Chief Chemist' rather than the names of the people.

## Colours alone do not always help

Multi-part sets are often made of papers of various colours − sometimes with instructions such as 'Pink copy to Stores', 'Blue copy to Sales Dept.' etc.

This is helpful if everyone can identify the colours. Unfortunately about one in seven of the male population in Western countries is in some degree colour blind and may not be able to differentiate between say, the red and the green copies.

## Letters – a frequent source of cost saving opportunities

Every business needs to write letters and the cost can be considerable. Reducing this cost starts with the question: 'Is your letter really necessary?'

If not, all or some of the following labour costs are avoidable:

● Composing the letter, e.g. a hand draft.
● Dictating to a secretary (which takes up the time of two people).
● Transcribing the shorthand or tape recording via a typewriter or word processor on to paper.
● Checking the typed letter (which may be altered and re-done) and signing it.
● Typing the address on an envelope, enclosing the letter and posting it.

plus

● Postage charges (1st class?).

An analysis of 1000 letters despatched by a London company showed that about 20% were probably unnecessary. These included acknowledgements of receipt, confirmations, and information which could have been included with other correspondence.

The company adopted a new policy, including:

1.    Not sending anything at all unless it was really necessary.

2.    Sending a pre-printed postcard in some cases, e.g. in acknowledgement of receipt.

3.    Using standard letters.

The third of these options resulted in some substantial savings. Careful study of old correspondence showed that, although the wording was different, there were many letters saying much the same thing.

Applying this to your company could reveal many standard situations requiring a standard reaction. These could include:

● Covering letters for quotations (and quotations themselves).
● Announcements of new products or services.
● Announcements of price changes.

- Chasing overdue payments.
- Confirmation of delivery dates – and the like.
- Acknowledgements of receipt of payments, reports, quotations and so on.

Standardised replies can be stored on a disk and produced via a word processor to give a 'personalised' letter. There is no need to emulate the old fashioned and clearly routine photocopy – which looks like a photocopy. Every letter from a WP will be an 'original', not a copy.

This saves time for all concerned and also reduces the chances of an error. Once correct on the disk the message will always be error free.

## Taking a look at your paperwork systems

This is another area where there are often substantial labour cost savings to be made.

The way in which we route paper is often the cause of delays and unnecessary work. The following is a chain of events based on a real-life case:

1. A new order is received (on an official company order form) by the order entry department.

2. The order is checked and the details copied on to a 4-part form – the order processing form.

3. The top copy of this form is clipped to the order form and filed in the order entry department. The remaining copies are distributed as follows:

    > 2nd copy to Accounts Dept;
    > 3rd copy to Sales Dept;
    > 4th copy to Records Dept.

4. Accounts department add a customer code and the price to be charged and send the form back to the order entry department.

    Sales department examine their copy and file it, having logged the product type and quantity ordered under a record by customer.

Records department record the product type and quantity ordered (for production planning purposes) and file copy number 4.

5. The order entry department, having received copy number 2 from the accounts department, check that the customer code and price have been added and then send the form to sales department.

6. Sales department, on receipt of copy number 2, check the price and attach a 'price approved slip'. They then send copy 2 back to order entry department who photocopy it twice.

   The photocopies are sent respectively to the despatch department and accounts.

   Accounts department prepare an invoice and a despatch note.

Confusing isn't it? In fact this is only part of the story but quite enough to illustrate the sort of self-imposed time – and money-wasters which can exist.

## What is wrong?

Quite a lot. First of all, we might ask why the customer's order (on the official company order form) needs to be copied on to an 'order processing form'. If an order form is suitably designed it could be used for all internal purposes as it stands.

Labour is wasted, delay incurred and the possibility of copying errors created by the use of the processing form.

The second most significant factor is the way in which copy number 2 is used. This copy *on which despatch and invoicing depends*, is sent first to the accounts department, then back to order entry department, then to sales, and finally back again to order entry.

In the real-life case on which this story is based, the total delay from receiving the order to doing something about it was sometimes as long as *three months*.

## Why the big delay?

Every time a piece of paper goes from one place to another it flops into someone's in-tray and joins a queue. Even if the work to be done requires only a few minutes, the paper can be static for a number of days waiting its turn. This is made much worse by absences due to holidays and sickness.

## Is your checking necessary?

The system described had a number of 'checks' built into it. Most checks are a waste of time. More often than not few errors are found; if there are lots of errors to 'justify' the check, there is probably something causing them. The causes should be removed rather than spend valuable resources on checking – and correcting.

### What else is wrong?

A number of actions can be queried. They are:

● The top copy of the processing form is filed in the order entry department and never sees the light of day again. Clearly this is a waste of paper and filing space.

● Recording the product type and quantity in both sales and records department is duplication of work.
   Records department is a candidate for being closed down – or merged into sales.

● At least one of the photocopies of copy 2 is unnecessary as copy 2 itself is merely filed and could have been sent to either despatch department or accounts instead of the photocopy.

● If accounts department know how to calculate the price (in fact a simple multiplication of quantity by unit price less discount) there is no need for sales to check it. The price has, in any case, already been checked by order entry department.

The problem is that such inefficiencies are not always easy to spot and since we are all used to the system it feels right. Most of the unnecessary to-ing and fro-ing will have been added bit by bit over the years – especially the checks, which tend to be leftovers from long retired managers who introduced them for reasons which were either invalid or are now extinct.

## Using a flow chart

The opportunities to improve matters can be revealed by using a flow chart such as is illustrated in Figure 7 on page 90.

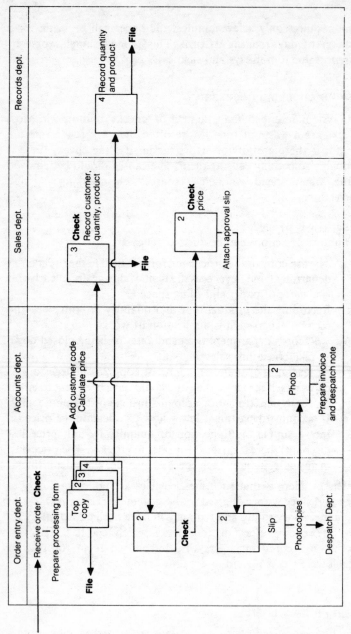

Figure 7. Using a flow chart to highlight opportunities to improve a system.

Once the chart is drawn, using colours for each department and symbols to represent bits of paper, any nonsenses can be more clearly seen. A useful measure is to have the chart examined step by step by each of the departmental managers concerned. Searching questions may be needed, such as:

- Why do you need a copy?
- Why do you check and what to do find?
- *When* do you need your copy?
- Why do *you* add the code number – why not someone else?

Questions such as these applied to the case described could well result in the order entry department being made part of the sales department – or at least being given authority to decide prices. This would cut out a lot of delay and improve customer service – in addition to other cost savings.

## SUMMARY OF KEY POINTS

1.  Paperwork costs money and bad paperwork can cost lots of money. Each badly designed form, report or whatever can create work, reduce customer service and cause confusion.

2.  A regular review of the company paperwork can remove or prevent losses. The review should start with the basic question: 'Do we *really* need this paperwork at all?'.

3.  Ask the key questions.

    - What useful action results from the paperwork?
    - Is any useful action possible?
    - What would we lose if the paperwork were scrapped?
    - What would we gain if it were scrapped?

4.  Use an X-Chart to analyse families of documents – looking for ways to reduce the number in use and to cut out duplicated effort.

5.  Have a good look at each form from a design point of view. Are your forms:

- Logical in sequence?
- Self-explanatory?
- Suited to the job and the place where they are used?
- Properly spaced?

etc.

6.  Can printing costs be reduced by cutting out non-essential features?

7.  Watch out for problems which can be caused by using colours and/or printing the names of individuals on a document.

8.  Analysis of the use of letters can result in savings. Are all your letters really necessary? Can you use standard letters (via a word processor) to save labour costs?

9.  The flow of paper in the business needs examination from time to time. Find out who does what, how, when and why. Illustrating what happens on a flow chart can reveal opportunities to save money.

# CHAPTER 6

# REDUCING STOCK HOLDING COSTS

If you are paying your bank 15% per annum interest charges on an overdraft and you have a stock of raw materials, finished products and general stores of £100,000, then you are paying £15,000 p.a. for the privilege of storing things.

This is in addition to other storage costs such as rent for the space and insurance premiums.

All in all your stock holding could be costing you as much as 20% of its value *each year*.

Even if you have no bank overdraft or other funding the cost is still high. The products in your warehouse represent money and if by waving a magic wand they could be turned into cash then the cash could be invested either in a safe security or in the business itself. If the business is making 10% profit per year then any cash injected into it could yield the same return.

The golden rule must therefore be − 'Store the minimum and keep it at the minimum'.

Naturally, the minimum must be concomitant with the essential needs of your business. Running out of finished product and being unable to complete a customer's order will not help your profits. Nor would bringing production to a halt through lack of raw materials. Whether buying-in or manufacturing in-house, the starting point for controlling the inventory is working out the quantity to order − and when.

## The economic order quantity

There are some complicated formulae for working out the most economical size of purchase orders and the size of production runs for stock items. The mathematics, whilst no doubt fascinating to theorists, are often beyond the needs of the practical business person and, thankfully, can be ignored in favour of some basic commonsense.

However, research by management scientists does help us by drawing attention to important factors which we may overlook in the hurly-burly of day-to-day business.

The costs associated with placing an order for supplies (and receiving them) include:

- Negotiating the price.
- The clerical work in preparing the paperwork.
- Unloading the goods, checking them and placing them in the warehouse.

All of these take time and manpower. Clearly, the more frequently goods and orders are received the greater the cost over a period of time. This suggests that a large order should replace a number of small ones. Another advantage of a large order is the possibility of receiving a bulk order discount from the supplier.

However, a large order means a high storage cost, including the interest value of the money tied up.

All this means that some calculation is necessary and the starting point could be to compare the various payment alternatives that your supplier might give you. The simplest and least favourable situation is the one in which you are paying say, 15% interest on a loan or overdraft and you pay cash on delivery for your purchases. In this case, assuming no discount for cash, you are paying the full interest charge with nothing to compensate it. So what happens if you buy on credit terms?

## Three variations on credit terms

### a. Monthly payment – no discount

In recent years the '30 days' payment term has, by default, extended to something more in the region of 60 or even 70 days. However for the purposes of calculation let us assume that you are making a monthly purchase worth £4000 and that payment must be made at the end of the month following the month in which the invoice is received. In other words you are getting about 1½ months free credit. What is this worth in terms of bank interest saved?

With a 15% charge on your loan the saving would be:

$$£4000 \times 15/100 \times (1.5/12) = £75$$

## b. Discount for early payment

Let us assume that you are offered a 2% discount for payment within 14 days (half a month) of the date of the invoice.

The discount will yield £80 (2% of £4000), giving a net payment of £3920.

If you forgo the discount and pay, as in case (a) after 1.5 months then your saving (on interest) would be £75. In this case the discount is hardly worth taking. However, higher rates of discount and/or different rates of interest charge will make a lot of difference. Working it out and not just jumping at the discount is highly desirable.

## c. Discount for bulk delivery

Suppose you are offered a 5% discount for orders of £8000 — double your normal order size. Assume that payment terms are as in case (a) allowing you 1.5 months to pay.

Your actual payment would be £8000 less 5% = £7600. A saving of £400.

You will of course pay interest on the £7600 over *two* months (you have bought two months supply) and the interest charge on this will be:

$$£7600 \times 15/100 \times 2/12 = £190$$

Your net saving will be £400 − 190 = £210.

If you decided not to place a bulk order and stuck to your normal £4000 order you would, with 1.5 months to pay, gain £75 in interest charge saving. The bulk discount is therefore more attractive.

Obviously there are many permutations of discount and interest charges and other aspects to consider but the value of actually working it out as it affects your business is clear. Purchasing costs and stock holding costs can be reduced and hence profits improved.

## Let the supplier take the strain

A useful method, which is often acceptable to suppliers and will save you money is to place a call-off order. A call-off order works on the basis that in exchange for placing a bulk order, say for six months' supply, the supplier will make part deliveries when called and yet give you a bulk order discount.

Invoicing follows delivery and payment is made only for the quantities delivered.

### The benefit to your supplier

The supplier gains by having advance knowledge of your requirements. This enables him better to plan his production runs and, for example, reduce set-up costs. In addition it will help him with *his* purchasing as he can more accurately calculate his needs for raw material or parts.

### The benefit to you

The buyer gains not only from the bulk discount but also avoids the problem of finding storage space for a large quantity − and paying the stock holding costs. This problem is placed on the shoulders of the supplier.

The buyer also reduces his chance of loss due to deterioration, damage and (to some extent) pilferage, since most of this will take place in the supplier's warehouse. However, obsolescence dangers loom larger and so does the lack of flexibility to try substitute products. On balance, though, the call-off system normally pays off.

## When do we order or call-off?

In addition to the question of how large our order should be is the one of how frequently should orders be placed. The two considerations are interdependent, but it is possible to place, say, 12 orders per year for 1 ton each time or, say, 24 orders per year for half a ton. The decision is likely to depend at least in part on the price terms that can be negotiated, but there will always be a stock holding cost to be minimised. This can be done by means of a simple calculation with the aim of reducing to zero the level of stock at the time that the next delivery is made. By doing this the *average* stock level is minimised.

The factors to be taken into account are:

- the rate of consumption of the stock; and
- the 'lead-time' expected to elapse between placing the order and receiving the goods.

An important further aspect is a level of safety to cater for the unexpected. This can take the form of a larger than usual lead-time, changed rates of consumption or a combination of both.

Let us assume that a manufacturer is using 10 tons of raw material each week. Deliveries normally take 2 weeks to arrive after the order is placed and he places an order for 40 tons every four weeks.

The stock levels on this basis will be:

### Stock level

| Start of week | 1 | 40 tons | (1st delivery) |
|---|---|---|---|
| " | 2 | 30 " | |
| " | 3 | 20 " | |
| " | 4 | 10 " | |
| " | 5 | 40 " | (Delivery of 40 tons made) |
| " | 6 | 30 " | |
| " | 7 | 20 " | |
| " | 8 | 10 " | |
| " | 9 | 40 " | (Delivery of 40 tons made) |
| | TOTAL | 240 | |

Average stock holding = 240/9 = *26.7 tons*

Suppose now our manufacturer decides to order smaller quantities at shorter intervals. If he decides to order only 20 tons each time, the picture will look very different:

### Stock level

| Start of week | 1 | 20 tons | (1st delivery *and* new order placed) |
|---|---|---|---|
| " | 2 | 10 " | |

| | | | | |
|---|---|---|---|---|
| " | 3 | 20 | " | (Delivery made and order placed) |
| " | 4 | 10 | " | |
| " | 5 | 20 | " | (Delivery made and order placed) |
| " | 6 | 10 | " | |
| " | 7 | 20 | " | (Delivery made and order placed) |
| " | 8 | 10 | " | |
| " | 9 | 20 | " | (Delivery made and order placed) |
| TOTAL: | | 140 | | |

Average stock holding = 140/9 = 15.6 tons.

By reducing his size of order but ordering more frequently the average stock level has been reduced by 41.6% – a reduction which should be reflected in a similar cost improvement.

In real life the situation is unlikely to be so neat and tidy. It is possible that both consumption rates and delivery lead-times will fluctuate. It would be prudent never to allow stock levels to fall to zero as would be the case in the two examples described, where the end of weeks 4 and 8 would show a stock-out.

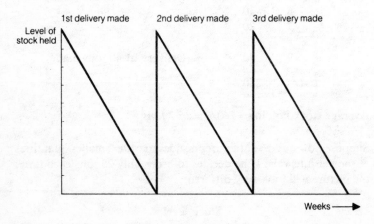

Figure 8. Minimizing the stock level.

However, the principle holds good that orders should be placed at a frequency designed to minimise stock levels i.e. as near as is practicable to 'just-in-time' deliveries. The concept is illustrated in Figure 8.

## Product for sale

The same just-in-time approach can be applied to producing goods for sale. Rather than stocking up the warehouse long in advance of making sales − and paying for the privilege − wherever possible an economic (production) order quantity should be worked out. In this case you will not be weighing up the stock holding savings against bulk order discounts or paying later rather than earlier, but against economies resulting from longer production runs and reduced set-up costs. Once again a safety stock may be necessary − this time to avoid failure to meet sales orders.

The factors that you must take into account will depend on the nature of your business, your market and your products.

### A historical note

Just-in-time (JIT) has become very much a buzz-word of recent years and the idea is widely credited to Japanese industries. In fact the whole business of economic order quantity and the JIT which goes with it was certainly understood as long ago as 1904 in the United States and has been described and referred to many times over the years.

## How much have we got?

Any system for ordering presupposes that we know what is in stock at any given time. This, as anyone who has worked in a production environment knows, is not always the case. The methods used to keep track of stock levels normally involve delivery and despatch notes, movement dockets, stock taking and a variety of recording systems ranging from the back of an envelope to a sophisticated computer system.

Data are moved by copying, or pressing keys on a keyboard, from bits of paper representing movements of materials and parts to a record. The record is then used by management to make decisions on ordering from production or buying in.

The sad fact of life is that such systems are expensive and unreliable. However well managed the system may be, the day will come when the computer printout or card index tells you that there are X items in stock – but only Y items can be found in the warehouse or store. This results from the inevitable human errors which will creep in. They can include:

- Miscounting during a stock check.
- Failure to check the amount said to be delivered.
- Despatching more than the required (and recorded) amount.
- Forgetting to record a stock movement or losing the docket.
- Delays in advising or recording a stock movement.

When the degree of error in the records reaches a level where problems are arising, e.g. production hold-ups due to lack of parts, more expense is incurred in stock taking and updating the records.

The fact is that in many situations recording systems are not necessary at all: the only true 'record' of what is on the shelves or floor is the stock itself. If, with *sufficient* accuracy you can measure the amount available, then all the elaborate recording systems can be scrapped.

## Visual stock control

A very simple case can illustrate the principle of visual stock control. The lady who runs the corner kiosk selling sweets, cigarettes, matches and odds and ends will probably not bother to keep any records – unless she works for some massive and bureaucratic organisation which insists on forms being filled in to tell them that the kiosk has a stock of 22 boxes of matches, 30 chocolate bars, etc., etc.

If she works independently she will not regard it as necessary to know her exact stock levels, only a rough figure for the purposes of placing a new order at the right time. She will find it by looking at the number of boxes of chocolate bars or whatever on her shelves. Her gut-feel for levels of sale will tell her that when she has, say, only two cartons of chocolate bars left, it is time to order more. She will receive a more positive reminder when she opens the last carton and again every time she takes a chocolate bar from it.

This visual method offers the following advantages:

1.   There are no paper or computer records or any need to reconcile actual stock figures with theoretical stock figures.

2.   There is a built-in mechanism to keep stocks as low as possible as orders will only be placed when essential and as a result of actual rather than forecast consumption.

The only other purpose for knowing the levels and values of the stock held is for year end return purposes when a stock-take will provide the necessary information.

Security is provided by reconciling takings with quantities ordered and the stock-take figure.

This system, with appropriate adjustments, can be used by virtually any business which holds stocks and can save a lot of cost and avoidable paperwork.

## More than a corner kiosk

Applying the visual control method to the vast majority of businesses will require rather more thought than is needed for the corner kiosk. However, the basic question will be the same: 'Why do we need to know how much stock we have?'

The answer is likely to be along the lines of ensuring that we don't run out when supplies are needed and making sure that we don't have too much. These needs can be met by the following procedure – which may need some adjustment for particular situations:

1.   Decide on the economic order quantity for the item concerned.

2.   Work out the amount of stock required to see you through the delivery lead-time and then a safety stock to allow for something going wrong.

3.   Set aside the amount of stock worked out under (2) and mark it in some way. One company does this using coloured adhesive tape which *effectively seals* the stock so that it cannot be used without breaking the tape.

   Examples from real life include:

   ● Bundles of metal and plastic piping stored in a yard and held together with tape.
   ● Pallets placed in a corner of the store with a coloured line painted on the floor to mark off the area and the pallets.

- Boxes of nuts, bolts, springs, washers and the like taped together.
- Barrels of liquid with coloured tape sealing the bungs.
- Small cans of liquid taped together in bundles.
- A shelf full of items and marked with red paint.

4.   Attach to the lead-time stock a ready-prepared purchase order made out for the calculated economic order quantity.

The storekeeper is now free to make issues from the unmarked stock (the free stock) without keeping any records. A stores requisition may be a necessary part of your way of working but this should be all that is needed in the way of internal paperwork. Once the free stock has been used up the storekeeper will start to use the lead-time stock. This is the trigger for him to take the pre-prepared order form and send it to the production department or a supplier. (Copies for the accounts department and anyone else who needs them can be included if required.)

If all goes well the lead-time stock will just be running out when the next delivery arrives. When this happens, a new lead-time stock must be set up along with a new purchase order.

## What happens if delivery is delayed?

However regular deliveries have been in the past the day will come when, as a result of strikes, adverse weather or some other cause, something will be delayed. In such cases the safety-stock comes into its own. As soon as the storekeeper needs to use it – or before if the lead-time stock is dwindling faster than usual – a signal is given to chase up the order. In serious cases an alternative source of supply may be urgently sought or a substitute product used. A warning can also be given to production planners or sales staff to enable them to take steps to avoid or limit any damage.

This, in practice, seems to work better with a visual system than those which rely on a computer print-out or other record which is subject to faulty input and delays in receiving it. It is not unknown for a computer report to be received some time after the absence of stock was glaringly obvious in the store or warehouse.

## Keeping the accountants happy

One of the major built-in advantages of the visual system is that free stock is used up and *only topped up* when really necessary. Indeed if everything goes perfectly (not likely, but possible) there will never be any free stock at all. The lead-time delivery will arrive just in time and the lead-time stock will keep things going. This means that there is a constant trend towards having lower stocks and thus lower costs. Any unnecessary free stocks which are lying around at the start of a visual system will be used up before any replacement is ordered. Experience has shown that significant cost reduction can result from this.

In addition to lower stock holding costs the accountants will be looking for a quick means to value stocks for the year end figures. Since (a) the amounts in the lead-time stocks are pre-arranged they need not be counted and (b) free stock quantities will always be moving downwards, there will be less stock taking to be done. Of course the accountants would find it easier to simply take a figure off the record − but it is often necessary to verify this by a physical stock check anyway.

## A variation on the theme

Not all stocks are held in stores and warehouses. There is almost always a percentage of raw materials, spares and so on in bins and boxes on the shop floor. There is a tendency in some companies to over-control such stocks − often as an attempt to prevent pilferage. Elaborate requisition systems may be used and rigid limits kept on the amounts issued. The usual result is a lot of to-ing and fro-ing from shop floor to store, a lot of supervision by foremen and, not infrequently, a hold-up while more bits and pieces are obtained from the storekeeper. Pilferage still goes on and no system has ever been devised which will wholly prevent it.

The answer is to allow each shop floor worker to control his own stock visually. Tubs of materials can be provided with, at the bottom of the tub, a plastic bag containing a lead-time stock and stores requisition. As soon as the bag is opened the requisition is sent to stores for another tub of materials. The free stock need not be counted or controlled and topping up becomes an 'automatic' process. Initially pilferage may increase until it is realised that desirable items are always available − when pilferage returns to its normal level. The only case where this is not a reliable conclusion is that of highly saleable items. In this case other controls may be necessary – often such measures as gatehouse checks which already exist.

## 80:20 again

Control on the shop floor can be based on the 80:20 rule. It is likely that a minority of items represent the majority of the value and/or a minority of items represent the things worth stealing. An analysis may indicate that costly control measures can be limited to a few items and abandoned for the rest. There is all the difference between a plain steel washer and a diamond-tipped drill bit.

# Reducing waste

Wastage of stock can arise from:

● Deterioration due to ageing.
● Deterioration due to damp or other environmental conditions.
● Bad handling causing damage.
● Contamination.

Any losses resulting from these or other causes are a direct charge on profits and, in many cases, avoidable. What is more, the causes are often known by warehouse staff, lorry drivers and the like but not by management, who grumble about the cost but accept it as unavoidable. It is often wholly avoidable and asking the employees what causes it – or better still, how to avoid it – can yield a profit. Consider these real-life examples:

## An unkind cut

A small company manufactured high-quality housewares which were injection moulded from a granular raw material. The granules were supplied in paper sacks.

There was a substantial wastage of finished products due to discoloration and other blemishes.

Complaints were made to the suppliers, who checked several samples of their product but could find no fault with it. After much time and effort the cause was discovered accidentally when the supplier's representative happened to see one of the moulding machine operators open a bag of granules. He cut the bag with a knife.

The effect of this was to cause small fragments of paper to fall into the granules. Although the contamination was slight it was enough to spoil some of the mouldings.

The supplier's bags were supplied with a special opening device to prevent such problems but no one had pointed this out to the machine operators, who continued an older practice of using a knife.

## Bending the rules

Long, narrow, metal containers were stored and distributed by a company in the Middle East. Many of the containers were found on delivery to customers to be distorted and unusable.

How the distortion occurred was a mystery until observations were carried out on the way in which the containers were handled. They were moved around in the warehouse by means of a forklift truck, the prongs of which were centrally positioned under the container before it was lifted. The result was that the ends of the containers, not being supported, sagged a centimetre or two resulting in the containers being bent.

A simple modification to the forklift solved the problem.

So what can be done to prevent losses from stock wastage?

The essential requirement is to work out, for each product involved, a sensible, safe way to store and handle it. This should be a positive act carried out routinely in order to save money and improve profits. It should not be left to chance. Some thought will be required, along with advice from suppliers and perhaps some trials. The responsibility for doing the job should be clearly allocated to an individual in order to reduce the chances of the work being overlooked.

Otherwise the following is a checklist of questions to ask:

- Are the stocks as *visible* as possible – enabling the state of them to be seen easily?
- How often do we inspect our slower-moving items for rust and other signs of deterioration?

- Are the buildings dry and clean?
- What is the best temperature in which to store our goods?
- Have we trained our people in proper handling methods?
- Are we using the right machinery for stock handling and movement?
- Do we know and regularly check the causes of wastage − or do we just shrug it off as unavoidable?
- Are liquids stored away from solids or goods otherwise separated to prevent cross-contamination?
- Do we have a means to guard against age deterioration such as a 'first in, first out' system?
- Do we regularly check to see if there is anything we should sell off at reduced price to cut losses?

## SUMMARY OF KEY POINTS

1. Any stocks you are holding represent money. This can be money you have borrowed and on which you are paying interest or the cash you would earn by selling the stock.

   The cash you would gain from sales also has an interest value − or the return you would get from investing it in your business.

   Stocks should therefore be kept at the lowest possible level.

2. Work out an economic order quantity to help keep stock holding costs to a minimum.

3. Try arranging a call-off system with your suppliers. This will reduce your financial burden.

4. Stock control can be an expensive activity. Try using a visual control system to reduce paperwork and clerical costs − and to help keep stocks at a low level.

5. Don't just accept losses caused by deterioration of stocks, contamination and other causes of waste. Find out why losses occur and take appropriate action.

6. Work through the checklist provided at the end of Chapter 6.

# CHAPTER 7

# *REDUCING DISTRIBUTION COSTS*

The term 'distribution' covers a multitude of functions. Some people might even include the design of special vehicles, packaging research and other such specialised subjects under distribution. This chapter deals with the 'primary' distribution activities 'which place the product or service where the customer wants it': that is, storing the product and then moving it to where the customer needs it to be − normally his own premises.

## Do service businesses have distribution costs?

The answer to this question is 'yes' − despite the absence of any tangible product. Some services such as hotels do have a form of tangible product including the meals, accommodation and other facilities provided to the traveller. These are not stored in the sense that a manufacturer will store his finished product before sending it to his customer. They are nevertheless placed where the customer wants them to be.

The location of Trust House Forte's Post House hotels is a first-class illustration. The product is no-fuss accommodation for business travellers and is strategically placed to be convenient to them. Post Houses are situated near motorways or other main roads, within convenient distance of city centres but not within the city.

Similar positioning of Travelodge and Happy Eater restaurants also illustrates the principle of putting what the customer wants where he wants it.

Purely service businesses such as banks and building societies place themselves in high street locations for the convenience of customers. It is probable that the choice of building society or bank, when an individual decides to open an account, is dominated as much by the location of the nearest branch as by the image and reputation of the society or bank concerned.

A well-known British company of insurance loss adjusters – providing no tangible product except a report of their findings – has offices strategically placed around the world. This enables them to provide a prompt service from staff with valuable local knowledge wherever a disaster or lesser loss may occur. Once someone has experienced a loss such as storm damage or a factory fire, both the owners of the property and their insurers want a fast assessment of the damage. Local offices can provide this information more quickly than the alternative of sending someone (who may not be immediately available) from some distant part of the world.

Clearly, these positional aspects of distribution have a strong sales element and form part of the marketing strategy – the costs of which are examined in Chapter 8.

## Distributing the tangible product

There are two main aspects to consider when a tangible product is involved:

- Where to store the product.
- How to move it.

Both involve significant cost and if not carried out effectively can wreck the business. Late deliveries can lose customers whilst an over-emphasis on customer service can create unsustainable costs. The decision as to what to do and what it should cost must start with the customer and his wants. However, an essential requirement is a dose of realism. Service is important and if a 24-hour delivery service is *really* necessary to compete then it must be provided. There have been cases, however, where the supplier *assumes* that a particular level of service is necessary and pays through the nose to provide it. When these same suppliers asked their customers what they wanted, they were surprised to hear that their assumptions were incorrect.

A real-life example came from the service industry where a company providing insurance services had a policy of 24-hour response to overseas clients. This level of service cost a lot of money to provide and involved a high level of staffing. When an overseas client commented that the rapid response was not in fact of any help the company asked other customers what they wanted. It was found that anything up to 72 hours was entirely satisfactory and office costs could be reduced.

It is also often possible, if the customer is consulted, to find ways and means to give him what he wants more cheaply. Routine deliveries, reserve stock on the customer's premises and larger or smaller package sizes are all possible arrangements which can suit your customer and save you money.

The effect of a slight reduction in service levels can be a major reduction in cost. As a *general* rule, increasing service levels from, say, 50% customer satisfaction to say 75% requires little extra cost. The same is not true if the increase is from, say 95% to 99%. To provide the extra 4% at this high level of service can involve the cost of such things as stand-by vehicles and drivers, very high levels of stock, and 'special' deliveries by courier — or even by air freight. The company which regularly sends a small package in a large lorry on a Sunday needs a very good reason to justify the costs; and pride in a superlative level of service is not sufficient justification.

This is not an argument against providing a good, competitive service. It is an argument against providing an unnecessarily expensive level of service caused by either an obsession with service or perhaps a lack of organisation and control.

A useful exercise is to look at the background to past 'special' deliveries:

● What did they cost?
● Were they profitable or did they make the sale into a loss?
● Why was it done?
● Could any of them have been avoided?
● What damage, if any, would have been done to the business if the special deliveries — or perhaps some of them — had not been carried out?

The answer to these queries may reveal a lack of cost awareness, inadequate costing procedures, poor planning — or simply panic action on someone's part.

## The practical but positive view

Having ascertained the realities of our situation − the real level of distribution service which must be provided and its cost − there is a management attitude which must be adopted. This is to regard distribution not as a painful matter of pure cost but as part of the product as a whole. Value can be added to a product by its distribution back-up and is virtually part of the design of the product.

Take the view that distribution is more than an expensive add-on: it is part of your whole marketing effort.

## Where do savings begin?

Distribution normally starts with storage. This is the first activity in which savings can be made. Assuming that your quantities are under control, the location of the stocks need to be examined.

In a production situation there will almost always be some element of storage at the production site − if only to accommodate the results of a production run which are waiting shipment to a customer or warehouse. Apart from this there are two broad alternatives for location with significant cost and service implications. They are:

● Centralised storage.
● Satellite storage.

The trick is to find the alternative which maximises service levels but minimises cost.

### The centralised option

Storage of products for sale in one, relatively large, location has the following potential advantages:

● Relatively easy stock level control by virtue of having only one place to check.
● Economies of scale, e.g. less labour cost per unit of stock held.

110

- Less handling of goods – and consequent losses resulting from damage.

The disadvantages can include:

- Longer delivery time.
- Higher transport costs.

Both, of course, arise from greater distance from the customer.

## The decentralised option

Storage in a number of satellite warehouses, strategically placed near to your main sales areas, can have the following advantages:

- Faster delivery to customers.
- Lower transport costs.

At first sight lower transport costs may appear to be unlikely, because goods must be transported first from the production site to the satellite warehouse and then, separately, to the customer. Whilst this will sometimes be the case it is also possible to send bulk deliveries in heavy vehicles to the satellite which in turn makes smaller-scale deliveries locally in smaller, more economical, vehicles. A fully loaded large vehicle delivering to the satellite is a cheaper proposition than a part-loaded vehicle delivering to a far-flung customer. However, it must be said that careful routing of a larger vehicle delivering from a central location to a number of customers can also be an economic proposition – if your customers have been so kind as to place themselves to make easy routing possible.

The disadvantages of decentralisation are:

- Greater difficulty in supervision and control.
- Increased handling.

The disadvantages can often be set against a potential major saving open to many businesses.

## A major saving possibility

A medium-sized company with its production facilities located in London stored its finished products in premises on the outskirts of the city. Considerable costs were regularly incurred in moving goods to customers in the Midlands and North of England, and there were some nail-biting occasions when there was no certainty that delivery would be made on time.

On one occasion, as a result of unusual circumstances, it was necessary to find a temporary storage facility in the North and a warehouse was rented in Yorkshire. This enabled the company to meet the short notice needs of a customer in Leeds, and, later, the needs of another in Scotland.

The temporary storage was at first seen as an unwelcome addition to distribution costs made necessary by the needs of two customers. However, it was also noticed that the cost of renting the warehouse was much less per square foot than for equivalent accommodation in the London area. The result was a re-evaluation of customer needs, transport and storage costs. It was calculated that substantial savings could be made by maintaining the barest minimum of storage in the London area and placing most of the stock in Yorkshire. At the time of writing the company is examining the advantages of a second satellite warehouse on the England/Wales border — a possibility made more attractive by lower employment costs in the region. In the meantime costings have shown that the difference in storage costs between regions is so great that it can be advantageous to transport goods from south to north and then back again to meet customer needs in the south.

The company is now seriously considering relocating its production facility as well.

This case study draws attention to some questions to be asked and answered:

● Can cheaper storage space be found elsewhere?
● Is there a cheaper location which will be more — or at least as — convenient for deliveries to customers?
● Even if the cheaper area is not convenient for some customers, is it still cheaper to store goods there despite any increase in transport costs?

## Is financial help available?

There are, in the United Kingdom, a number of regions keen to entice businesses to move to them. Local high levels of unemployment are often the reason for seeking to encourage immigrant businesses, and in these so-called Development Areas grants and loans are available. In the financial year ending March 1989 a total of £44.3 million was made available by the Department of Trade and Industry and local development corporations add other incentives. Why not take advantage of this?

Rent and rates concessions can be obtained and, in addition, grants of up to 100% can be obtained for parking facilities, 90% for buildings and 50% for conversions. Such benefits can make the costing of decentralised services very attractive, providing a significant contribution to cost reduction and a more attractive bottom line figure.

If, at the same time, decentralised storage can result in faster delivery to customers, then an edge on the competition will be gained – possibly resulting in more business and economies of scale.

## Shifting the goods

Your product can be moved either by yourself or by someone else – or a mixture of the two.

Which of these is the best choice depends on a number of factors, including:

- The nature of your products.
- The relationship with your customers.

A company selling fragile and perishable goods such as cut flowers or soft fruit may well be reluctant to hand over its deliveries to a contractor. The same might apply to a business which develops a close personal relationship with customers. An example might be a company in the catering trade supplying restaurants, public houses and small hotels. The driver of the delivery vehicle could well be expected to learn the various preferences of the customers, times at which delivery is unwelcome and also act as an order-taker for future deliveries.

Conversely, a producer of bulky and robust goods such as metal ingots or garden furniture may find it an advantage to use a contractor.

The advantages of doing it yourself are:

- Greater control over deliveries and timing.
- Ability to offer a more personal service.

The advantages of using a contractor include:

- No worries about vehicle maintenance, renewal of insurances, breakdowns and repairs, etc.
- No necessity to employ drivers – and to ensure that they do the job properly.
- No vehicle costs are being incurred during periods when they are under-used.

The value of these opposing advantages will vary from business to business and must be weighed up against the costs of the two alternatives.

## What is the cost of doing it yourself?

Providing your own transport will incur certain unavoidable costs *and* offer cost alternatives.

The ways to provide your own transport services include:

- Buying vehicles outright.
- Leasing.
- Hiring.

In the case of buying vehicles outright you will have to allow for the full range of expenses:

- Depreciation.
- Tax and insurance.
- Repair and maintenance.
- Garaging.
- Employment of drivers.

If the vehicles are leased the depreciation cost is avoided and if vehicles are hired all the costs listed are avoided except the wages of the drivers.

Choosing between the three options is a fairly complex calculation involving, among other things, tax considerations. The position regarding tax is subject to change, depending on the whims of the politicians who will move the goalposts from time to time, and must be checked.

114

## Avoiding capital expenditure

Leasing and hiring also avoid the problem of finding a large capital sum which may have to be borrowed from a bank at a painful rate of interest – plus an 'arrangement fee' and other charges which banks are fond of.

Paying a monthly leasing charge at least avoids this cost and also makes cash-flow forecasting easier. There is, however, likely to be a penalty clause in the leasing contract which is payable if the lessee wants to pull out before the term of the contract has expired. Against this the contract may allow the lessee to exchange the vehicle originally leased for a newer one before the lease has run its course – still without having to find new capital.

## The cost per mile calculation

Comparing the net cost of buying, leasing or hiring is fairly complex but is made easier and more realistic if the whole thing is reduced to a cost per mile calculation.

If, say, your total fixed costs of a vehicle purchased outright are £1000 per month and you do an average 1000 miles per month, then your cost per mile is £1 plus fuel costs.

If the cost of hiring a similar vehicle works out at, say, £800 per month, then your cost per mile works out at 80p per mile.

There will be a break-even point below which hiring is cheaper and above which ownership is cheaper. The same applies to leasing and its comparison with other methods.

## Fleet management – another alternative

Companies which need a number of vehicles might consider sub-contracting the administration of them to a professional firm of fleet managers. The following are some of the services offered by fleet management companies:

- Acquisition of new vehicles – with the advantage of bulk purchasing power.
- Maintenance and repair – again with the cash advantage of greater purchasing power.
- Selling old vehicles – where expertise should result in a better than average second-hand price.

A good firm of fleet managers will offer cost savings and removal of much of the hassle which looking after vehicles can involve. Of course they charge fees for their work, but this should be more than covered by, say, lower purchasing costs.

## A 'total' alternative for distribution

Your business may lend itself to sub-contracting your whole distribution activity to a specialist company.

Commonplace in the publishing world, this means handing over your finished product to a sub-contractor who will store it and ship it to your customer.

The sub-contractor thus takes on the whole burden of providing warehouse space and vehicles *and* the management of them. There is always the danger that the sub-contractor will not meet the service standards you need, and checking them out combined with clear, written, standards are essential – before the contract is signed.

Whether or not the sub-contractor's charges are a better option also needs to be worked out. But even if the sub-contracting option is more expensive, the difference may be worth paying to avoid the management time and energy involved in doing it yourself. The time released could perhaps be better applied in other areas of your business.

### SUMMARY OF KEY POINTS

1. Distribution – putting your product or service where the customer wants it – should be regarded as a critical factor in your marketing package.

2. The two main aspects of distribution, and the areas where savings should be sought, are:

   ● Deciding where to store your product.
   ● Deciding how to move your product.

3. Start with the customer and his needs when making decisions

on storage and transport, but be realistic – unnecessary levels of service bring about unnecessary levels of cost.

For example, analyse those 'special deliveries'. Were they justified or even necessary?

4. Examine the pros and cons for your business of centralised storage and satellite storage. You may find that the lowest cost option meets all your customer service needs.

5. Is it cheaper and practical to store your goods in a low rent area – even if this means increased transport and handling costs?

6. Can you benefit from grants and concessions by placing your storage in a development area?

7. Calculate the cost difference between running your own transport system and contracting it out.

8. If you prefer to run your own transport look at the alternatives of purchase, lease and hire. The cost difference could be considerable.

A cost per mile calculation is the best way to compare costs.

9. Shop around for alternatives – including fleet management services.

10. Consider the 'total alternative' – sub-contracting your whole distribution requirement.

# CHAPTER · 8

# REDUCING MARKETING COSTS

Advertising, market research, participating in exhibitions and other promotional activities can amount to one of the most expensive items in a company budget.

Enthusiasm for these marketing approaches can easily go out of control – particularly if sales are falling and a degree of panic creeps in.

Considerable care and thought need to be applied to marketing, starting with the decision as to what form is appropriate to your business and will produce value-for-money results.

## Marketing research

Many companies carry out market research from time to time. Fewer, it seems, conduct any form of market*ing* research to find out which are the best ways of promoting the business and its products. Money spent on ineffective marketing is wasted money.

What does marketing research involve? Essentially, it is a process of asking basic questions about alternative methods to find out how they relate to potential customers.

Let us take advertising as an example. The many options include:

Local press
National press
Trade journals
Street hoardings
Television
Radio

Some of these are relatively cheap, some very expensive; by no means all are going to influence your potential customer.

Questions need to be asked and answered for each of the options, including:

- How many people will be likely to see the advertisement?
- What sort of people are they? Are they the sort of people who will want to buy your product?
- What will the cost be per potential customer reached?
- What message must be put across in your advertisement in order to influence the type of people who will see it? What matters to them?

## Comparing various methods

You may decide that advertising in a particular medium will produce value-for-money results. Before going ahead, it is worth making a comparison with the likely costs and results of using quite different methods.

Other marketing techniques to consider include:

- Inviting potential clients to hear a presentation, while they enjoy a buffet lunch or supper.
- Telephone contact.
- Direct mail, using a carefully chosen mailing list.
- Personal referrals, e.g. obtaining the help of satisfied customers.

All these methods have their own characteristics and costs, but they generally offer greater precision than advertising. Presentation seminars, for example, tend to be expensive, but they allow you to control the composition of your audience.

## Another possibility

Taking a stand at an exhibition is another marketing option. The cost need not be ruinous if elaborate stands are avoided and some advice is taken from a consultant or other expert in the field.

Among the requirements for a successful exhibition appearance are:

- Careful choice of the right event, that is, one which is certain to attract the sort of people you w int to reach.
- Stand staffed by people who are trained in how to do it – and how not to do it.
- A simply designed stand which will put over your message at first glance and be positively welc ）ming to visitors.

Research will be needed into the eveits available and how you should use them, if at all.

## Building a strategy

The end result of all your research should be a strategic marketing plan which makes best use of your marketing budget.

Ideally, you will be working to a measurable objective, such as:

- To obtain 20 more major customers by a given date. (Definition of 'major' will be needed.)
- To increase sales revenue by X% by a given date.

or

- To reduce the cost of sales by Y% and/or the cost of obtaining a new customer by Z%.

## How not to do it

Without the research and thought required to produce a marketing strategy, some expensive mistakes can be made.

### The wasted advertisement

A three-man company manufacturing made-to-order shop fittings and general commercial joinery reached a critical cash-flow position. Sales had fallen off, and looking ahead a period of negative cash-flow could be foreseen. With only limited discussion and consideration it was decided to mount an advertising campaign in local newspapers and one trade journal. Precious funds were paid out for a number of small block-ads and also for a year-long contract for a monthly advertisement in the trade journal. The result? Absolutely nothing.

The payments on the monthly contract hung like the proverbial albatross round the necks of the proprietors, who were baffled by the lack of response.

Analysis of what they had done revealed the following facts about their advertising campaign:

- Most of the readers of the local newspaper advertisements would not be likely to be customers.

    It was reckoned that well in excess of 90% of the readers would be unlikely to be interested in the products on offer.
- The trade magazine would be read primarily by others in the same business and not by the customers of such businesses. The simple principle that candlestick makers don't buy candlesticks was overlooked.

Having failed to attract business by means of the advertising the proprietors then launched into further ill-considered action.

## The wasted salesman

It was decided that employing a full-time salesman would bring the results required. Money was borrowed, a salesman recruited and a company car provided. The salesman was sent out into the world after a bare minimum of briefing and the proprietors waited for the orders to roll in. They did not and after a month the salesman was (expensively) disposed of.

### What went wrong?

Firstly, the salesman had no prior knowledge of the business or its products. Even when he gained a hearing from a potential customer he was unable to give price quotations without referring back to one of the proprietors. This meant that a number of potential sales went cold while estimates and costings were being worked on.

Secondly, no attempt had been made to target the most likely customers. The salesman had travelled far and wide cold-calling on all and sundry. Most of his time had been wasted on the wrong people.

The irony of the situation was that the three proprietors had little to do themselves as a result of falling orders and, although they were primarily production men, one of them could have tried his hand at selling. This at least would have meant that someone who understood the products and could quote prices promptly would have done the talking.

It would also have saved the cost of the salesman's salary.

## Is there any misplaced marketing activity?

One of the common features of the smaller company is that marketing activity − selling and advertising in particular − is maintained at a level proportional to the number of existing customers. This is normally the result of setting a budget for marketing as a percentage of turnover or the value of orders received. At the same time, much of the marketing effort is directed at the existing customers rather than at entirely new prospects.

The result is wasted money and lost opportunities. Marketing effort should be directed at untapped segments of the market and should be proportional to expected sales.

The first requirement is to examine where the effort is going and the results of that effort.

For example it could be the case that, say,

● 60% of customers represent only 10% of revenue.
● 70% of calls made by salesmen are to customers who provide only 15% of sales.
● 40% of products produce only 5% of revenue.
● 30% of customers yield 70% of the profits.

If your analysis produces results such as this a number of possible courses of action can be considered.

## Some of the money-saving options

● Arrange that the great majority of salespeoples' time is concentrated on major accounts only.
● Organise carefully controlled calls on *potential* customers who could place orders of a significant size. Set a standard such that a potential customer will only receive prime

attention if his orders are likely to represent say 5% or more of sales revenue. There is no point in travelling 50 miles to talk to someone whose potential orders represent only a negligible amount of extra business.

● Deal with small customers by telephone or mail.
● Consider using sales agencies and freelance salespeople working on commission only.

A sales agency could be the best way for you to market your product overseas, and freelance salespeople may be able to deal best with smaller customers. In both cases your payments would depend on results and you would not be risking precious working capital.

By measures such as these the best use is made of human and other resources and experience shows that conscious, planned concentration on potentially large customers tends to increase sales and profits.

However, at this stage we are looking at ways to save money by eliminating waste as well as cutting down on expenditure. Spotting the waste in marketing requires constant monitoring of results of work done and learning the lessons which are presented.

## Ways to monitor the cost and results

A number of ratios can be selected to spot the good results (in order to exploit them to the maximum) and the bad results (in order to rectify the situation).

Possible ratios include:

● The number of orders received as a percentage of calls made.
● Average order values by salesperson.
● Sales costs as a percentage of sales order value. (Include all travel costs in this calculation.)
● Percentage of calls resulting in orders.
● Average number of successful calls per month.

Ratios such as these will indicate which salespeople are producing results and which not. They may also indicate that some geographical areas are worth concentrating on and some not.

A similar approach should be taken to advertising costs and, wherever possible, records kept of sales or enquiries resulting from advertisements. It is often not easy to link an advertisement with enquiries which result but the question 'how did you hear of us?' is worth asking. The answer gives an indication of which journals and/or styles of advertisement are bringing results and which not.

Once the fruitful media are identified the others can be dropped and money saved. Alternatively, coupon advertisements or mail shots enclosing a reply card are easy to monitor in terms of results achieved.

## The principles – in summary

Ask yourself what results are achieved for each pound spent on your marketing activities.

Find out which areas of activity are the most productive and which the least productive. By concentrating resources on the former your marketing will be less expensive per unit of revenue achieved.

### SUMMARY OF KEY POINTS

1. Marketing is expensive and warrants analysis to find out which methods etc. will pay off best.

2. Marketing research should be used to devise a value-for-money strategy.

3. Analyse your sales by salesperson, area, revenue, profit and so on.

4. Concentrate on accounts which have the greatest potential and find cheaper ways to deal with small accounts.

5. Monitor results carefully in order to identify the marketing methods which work best and then concentrate on them.

# PART THREE

# Increasing Revenue

CHAPTER · **9**

# *SHORT-TERM THINKING*

The simplest way to increase revenue is to increase sales turnover –
and the simplest way to do that is to cut prices. However, this could
have a devastating effect on profits and the temptation to reduce
prices should be resisted. Only if the most careful analysis and
calculation results in clear and positive favourable indications
should price reduction be considered.

## Raising prices

In some businesses such as perfumery and clothing an *increase* in
price can result in more sales. This results from the 'snob-appeal'
of high-priced products and the creation of greater demand from a
narrow segment of the retail market.

The fear of losing business and reducing profits as a result of
raising prices can be exaggerated. Many small business people have
found that a *sensible* increase will be accepted by customers and
this should be considered. An increase reflecting the rate of
inflation should be justifiable, and there is no argument for
carrying on if your price does not cover your costs.

There are, fortunately, other ways to increase sales turnover
which involve less risk.

## To discount – or not to discount

Giving a discount either for prompt payment or for large orders is
a way to reduce your price without wrecking your price structure
overall.

The discount offered must be very carefully calculated to ensure that savings you gain by prompt payment, or perhaps lower unit delivery costs, at least equal the amount 'given away'.

Many buyers will respond to a discount – even a small one – and your overall profits can be improved. This is especially so if you are borrowing at a high rate of interest.

## Other inducements

All short-term measures will need to be simple and easy to arrange and, hopefully, will have a more or less immediate impact. Some of the following ideas, all successful in real life, might suit your business:

● *Give them something*
  For a month every customer of a small engineering business was given a small but good quality pocket knife marked with the company name and telephone number.

  Old hat? Certainly, but such things work. It is no accident that airlines will give a present worth a pound or two to first-class passengers. The satisfaction of a small gift is out of all proportion to its cost and does encourage repeat business.

  Hotels have discovered that presenting a few fancy chocolates to their guests can result in more sales. The travelling business executive puts them in his briefcase and gives them to his children when he gets home. Their pleasure may remind him to use the same hotel next time he travels.

  One hotel chain is extra generous with bathroom supplies of body lotion and the like. The increasing numbers of female executives travelling on business has not been overlooked – nor has the fact that some male travellers will take the toiletries home to their wives. On the basis of such minor differences as a larger bottle of good quality body lotion the choice of hotels is made.

● *Competitions*
  An international insurance company designed a competition which could be entered by the brokers who brought in new business. A cash prize was offered for the broker who suggested the best idea for preventing losses – and hence the

127

claims which the insurance company would otherwise have to pay.

This idea not only drew attention to the company and its products, but also opened up the possibility of finding ways and means to reduce losses.

● *Referrals*
One small business has increased sales by the simple expedient of giving every satisfied customer two of its business cards with a request that one be passed on to someone else with a recommendation. Cheeky? Maybe, but it works. If only one customer in ten does anything about it, the result can be significant; and any recommendation is worth a lot of exhortation in expensive advertisements.

The idea of 'paying' customers to introduce others is also finding wider applications. A free year's subscription to a magazine, a gift or even the chance to enter a draw for a free holiday are some of the carrots offered.

● *Special offers and slow movers*
'Get three for the price of two' or 'Free nail brush with every bottle of bath oil' are familiar types of offer in the retail sector. They can have substantial advantages in addition to producing a surge of revenue. The nail brush, or its equivalent in your business, could be a slow-moving stock item which is costing you money to store. Ideally, the 'free' nail brush will be costed into the price of the combined product offer so that a profit overall will be made. At worst break-even should be achieved plus the saving on stock holding costs.

The 'three for the price of two' offer can also be a way of clearing slow movers, but both types of offer have the additional advantage of drawing attention to your business.

## Is the skip full of your money?

Almost everything that is manufactured has waste products associated with it. Thousands of tons of broken glass, metal shavings, sawdust, off-cuts, 'flash' from plastic mouldings, scrap paper, rag, used oil, contaminated chemicals, unwanted containers, and even expensive wood pallets find their way into rubbish dumps.

At the same time, almost everything which is rubbish to one business is a raw material to another. Alternatively your business may be able to find a way to use its own waste. If you can find a way to sell your waste and/or convert it economically into a saleable product you are in effect getting your raw material or product for nothing.

Too often the subject of waste is neglected or ignored. No attempt is made, say, to find a buyer for by-products or to recover and recycle them. It is all too easy to dump it and forget it.

One small business found someone to buy small quantities of scrap metal and another purchaser for rather larger quantities of scrap timber. Neither of these deals produced a great deal of money but a fair degree of sales turnover was represented by it. If you can gain £100 per month for your rubbish, this could represent a £1000 sale in terms of net revenue. You may also be relieved of the cost of paying someone to remove the rubbish.

## Do you have spare capacity?

A vehicle standing in your car park or a machine switched off for several hours a day are resources for which you are paying and which are earning you nothing. Even if you cannot use them yourself, can you sub-contract their capacity to someone else?

Spare capacity on a lathe, a milling machine, a word processor – even some unused space in your store – are all potential money earners and should not be left unexploited.

Sometimes spare capacity becomes available on a regular basis because of a seasonal pattern for sales. If there is a clearly definable cycle then, in addition to any possibilities of sub-contracting, another product should be sought which can fill the gaps. A company with a seasonal fall-off in July and August used their machines to make high-quality wooden toys which were sold to local retailers and at craft fairs. The profit was small, but earnings were more than enough to pay the cost of otherwise under-used labour and equipment. Thus a seasonal loss was turned into a profit.

## Direct marketing – a rapidly expanding method

No one knows who first invented direct marketing; the method probably goes back to the earliest days of the use of writing. It is known, however, that over 200 years ago Benjamin Franklin sent a catalogue by post to potential customers of his bookselling business. Franklin had hit on the notion that if the customers could not come to him and he could not go to them, a catalogue would bridge the gap and widen his market.

Direct marketing has grown enormously since Franklin's day and in the USA adds up to business worth around 20 billion dollars a year. Sales by direct means have doubled in Europe during the 1980s and are on the increase in the Far East and other regions of the world. Nor is direct marketing limited to mailing catalogues. Television advertisements which include the use, in the UK, of the 0800 telephone numbers and telephone sales are other ways to reach a wider market.

Generally, such methods are cheap when compared with employing a sales force and can also replace normal advertising. In other words your precious sales budget can be switched wholly or partly to direct sales – the costs need not be additional to the traditional newspaper or magazine advertising campaign.

### Another advantage

The other advantage of direct marketing is that it can enable you to reach far-away markets, e.g. overseas, which might otherwise be both expensive and difficult to penetrate. The smallest company can afford at least a limited amount of selling by mail to a far-away country when resources of time and money are insufficient for personal visits.

This point has not been missed by Royal Mail International in the UK, who are advertising their services in respect to the 1992 European single market. This advertising includes the statement: 'International Direct Mail will allow you to exploit comprehensive business mailing lists across the continent ... you can reach Europe double-quick at the right price ... the International Business Reply Service brings business back to you by making it easy for your clients to respond.'

Should you decide that your product is suitable for direct marketing, and in particular if this will open up new sources of revenue, it should form part of your long-term thinking. Preparation, including careful selection of target areas, will be required and gearing up in a number of ways (administration, stock holding, etc.) will be needed.

The reward could be substantial as it has been for people in the financial services industry over the 1980s. The travel industry, publishers and the various charities are also growing users, and according to the *Financial Times* (18 April 1990) the 22 largest telemarketing companies had reached sales levels of about £50 million.

## Making it easy to buy your product

Some businesses make it very difficult to buy what they are offering. Sometimes this is brought about by a time barrier such as that which UK banks are now belatedly waking up to. If the bank is closed at the time when customers (who have jobs to do) want to do business, the banks will lose. This has benefited competitors such as building societies, who have always been prepared to do business on Saturdays. Now that the UK banks have lost billions overseas they must make it up at home and, lo and behold, they are beginning to open on Saturdays also.

Small businesses cannot afford to make this kind of mistake.

### Other barriers to bring down

There are other barriers placed in the way of customers, and some are very common.

How many of these responses ring a bell?

- We cannot take orders over the phone.
- You must fill in our official order form.
- We do not deal with personal callers.
- Please get in touch with our agents.
- This is the head office, you must contact our nearest local branch.

There is a British company which offers a first-rate product. They advertise that it is only necessary to call them on the telephone and all you want will be yours. This would be fine if their sales staff were trained to deal with calls in the way the *customer* wants (rather than the company way), so that they get the order right and send out confirming paperwork which is both understandable and correct. The time actually required to place an order and then to sort out the only too frequent muddles does nothing to encourage further business.

In other words, 'You don't count Mr Customer, our laid-down procedures are paramount.'

## How to lose a customer

A customer buying some clothing in a well-known chain store offered a cheque for payment backed up by a cheque card which more than covered the price. The sales assistant accepted the cheque and the card, but insisted that the purchaser's address must be written on the back of the cheque and be *supported by proof of address*.

As the customer could not supply proof of address, the sale was refused. Although the supervisor agreed that the cheque card guaranteed the payment, proof of address was required as it was 'company policy'.

The result? A lost sale and a permanently lost customer.

### SUMMARY OF KEY POINTS

1.  Don't be tempted to reduce prices in an attempt to increase turnover − unless you have *sound* evidence that it will work. You may be better off as a result of raising prices − a prospect to be looked at fearlessly.

2.  Consider discounts − for bulk orders or prompt payment (or both) − as a means to improve profits. But do work out the discount levels which will be beneficial. Don't just pick a number from the air.

3.  Look for inexpensive ways to promote your company and its products and to encourage customer loyalty, e.g. giveaways, competitions.

4. Have a look at what you throw away. How much did it cost you to buy it in the first place? Can you sell it? Can you re-process it?

5. Have you any spare capacity – people, machines, space – which you can put to good use?

6. If your business is cyclical (e.g. seasonal) examine the opportunities for maximising your resources in the 'trough' period. Should you diversify to make more profit from any under-used capital or other assets?

7. Direct marketing may offer you an opportunity to penetrate new markets – relatively cheaply and quickly.

8. Look for ways to make it easier for people to do business with you.
   Look at it from the customer's viewpoint and see if you are placing obstacles in his way to your door.

# CHAPTER 10

# IMPROVING YOUR SALES FORCE

## How good are your salespeople?

Some people, mistakenly, assume that good salespeople are born not made. Certainly there are people with the natural charm, convincing manner and oral fluency which predispose them to being able to sell. However these are also the characteristics of the con-man and do not alone make a good salesperson. There are a number of techniques to be used in successful selling which can be taught. Whether or not your salespeople need this tuition will be indicated by the answers to these questions:

Do your salespeople:

- Talk too much and listen too little?
- Offer products/services or *solutions to customers' problems*?
- Work from the customer's viewpoint and make it obvious that they are doing so?
- Know the difference between the *features* of your products and the *benefits* for the customer resulting from those features?
- Identify the benefits which are relevant to the customer's needs and situations?
- Explain the benefits in the customer's terms?
- Know how to prepare for and start a selling interview?
- Know how to close a sale?
- Avoid seeing buyers as adversaries?
- Demonstrate commitment to customer satisfaction?
- Know how to deal effectively with complaints?

If the answer to any of these is unsatisfactory — or you do not know what the satisfactory answer should be — then there is a need for sales technique training.

The right training can substantially increase the effectiveness of salespeople and with it the revenue created from more sales and larger sales. Don't make the mistake of assuming that because someone has 'been on the road' for many years that they have learned it all. Many of the old sweats can improve their performance by adding to their experience techniques which need to be structured in use rather than applied instinctively.

## Get rid of bad practices

Some of the common bad practices which should be rooted out include:

● *Lack of detailed product knowledge*
All your salespeople should know their product inside out. Not only will this enable them to answer customers' questions confidently and convincingly, it will also reduce the risk of their giving the customer a misleading answer, and it will better enable them to spot and seize sales opportunities.
   Detailed product knowledge is essential to being able to identify real benefits to the customer and to explain them to him.

● *Lack of customer knowledge*
Failure to spot opportunities can also result from not knowing enough about the customer's business.
   A British company provided a service to a German company for over three years before it was discovered − accidentally − that the customer had a subsidiary company which could have used the same service. The customer had not realised that the service would have been applicable to his subsidiary company and had not mentioned its existence.
   Every available detail of your customer's operations, products, staff and who he sells to should be actively sought. Even his advertisements in trade journals can tell you something about him.

● *Concentrating on a few pet customers and failing to develop others*
It is far easier to call on people we know and from whom we get regular orders. Some salespeople will make themselves

very busy with pet customers when they should be developing new ones. Set your salespeople a monthly target for making new contacts.

- *Wasteful travel*
Poor scheduling can result in fewer calls and in almost every case the number of sales will be directly proportional to the number of calls made.
  Check how salespeople plan their work.
- *Unprofitable sales*
Some companies fail to make their salespeople aware of the size of order or other requirements which will make an order a profitable one.
  Have you found out what constitutes a profitable order in your company?

## Sales team supervision – a foundation for good results

Unsupervised or badly supervised people rarely produce the best results possible. In selling, a particular type of supervision is needed. Above all the supervisor needs to be aware of what the salesperson is doing and how he or she is doing it.
  The supervisor must ask:

- How many calls does each salesperson make and what proportion result in orders?
- Are too many calls made to allow time to do a proper job?
- How much preparation do salespeople make before calling on customers and prospects?
- Are post and telephone used to keep in touch with customers?
- Are complaints given priority and sufficient attention to ensure that they are cleared up *to the customer's satisfaction*?
- Is enough time spent on prospecting for new customers?
- Is time wasted on poor prospects which will never be likely to yield a worthwhile return?
- Do salespeople support each other, e.g. by referrals and passing on information about other people's customers or prospects?
- Does each salesperson set objectives – and/or agree objectives with the supervisor?

Ideally, every salesperson will be so well trained in preparation, time management and so on that they can do their jobs with minimum supervision. But some supervision will always be needed and not even the best salespeople out on the road should be 'out of sight out of mind'.

## SUMMARY OF KEY POINTS

1. Check the skills of your salespeople. Some good quality training in sales technique might work wonders for your sales turnover.

2. Root out weaknesses such as inadequate product or customer knowledge, concentrating on pet customers or wasteful travel plans.

3. Apply some effective supervision to your sales operation — setting standards and monitoring performance.

# CHAPTER 11

# PROVIDING MORE FOR YOUR CUSTOMERS

You will have a number of existing customers, sales outlets, storage facilities, transport or whatever is appropriate to your particular business. You will also have an existing range of products and services.

What can be done with these to increase your sales? Anything that you can do to increase sales without changes in product or increasing sales expenditure is likely to be a profitable way to make progress.

## The customer viewpoint

If you know how your customers view your company and its products you are in a strong position. This knowledge will enable you to spot opportunities to increase sales — possibly with only minor changes and at low cost.

It is often the case that business people can go on for a long time, even years, unaware of the views and opinions of the people with whom they do business. The difficulty is that they often *think* they know and make no effort to check that their beliefs are accurate. A little market research can be worth its weight in gold.

## Look for opportunities

When visiting customers, you can do more than just talk to the buyer or whoever normally places orders. Ask to have a look at the way in which the customer uses your products − perhaps by a walk round his factory floor. Talk to machine operators, warehouse staff and anyone else who comes into contact with your product. You may find that:

● You have other products or services which the customer is not buying but could use to his advantage.

> One such case concerned the use of a type of paint. The customer used the paint as a finishing coat on metal drums which had been treated with a type of bitumen. In discussion with the production foreman it was learned that the paint did not always produce a satisfactory finish. The supplier pointed out that the bitumen would inhibit a good finish and that the supplier's own undercoat, which was chemically compatible with the paint, would produce the right result − and be easier to apply than the bitumen.
>
> The customer had not known that the undercoat was available and the supplying company, having never enquired how their paint was used, had never offered it. Once the information had been exchanged sales of the undercoat commenced.

● There are other ways in which the customer can use products that he *does* buy from you.

Does he know that your de-greasing fluid can also be used as a paint stripper?

Is he aware that you provide a training service in addition to your main business?

● Changes to packaging or labelling could result in more sales.

● A change to delivery arrangements may help the customer and encourage him to buy more.

Anything that you can find − looking at it from the customer's point of view − which makes your company, your products or service more attractive and beneficial is likely to increase orders.

## Get your customer to visit you

Let him see your production facilities or discuss the administration side (invoicing, order placing, etc.) on site. Show that you are interested in *his* needs and problems and demonstrate that you are prepared to make changes which will help him.

You will probably find that some very small changes on your part, which cost you little, will be worth a lot to your customer and give you an edge over your competitors.

Some real-life examples are:

- A coloured self-adhesive label stuck on bags of product to indicate its age. This saved the customer from keeping a record of the age of the products in his store.
- An extra copy of the invoice marked 'copy' and sent direct to the customer's quotations department. This was helpful to the estimators who were encouraged to stipulate the supplying company's products in their quotations.
- Instruction booklets with spiral bindings so that they would lie flat on a work bench. In this case the spiral binding was cheaper than the glue binding which the supplier had used hitherto. Not only was the customer's need met but it saved money as well.

## Bacon and egg possibilities

There are many cases where the purchase and use of one product demands the purchase and use of another. These are the 'bacon and egg' situations we should look for. Common examples are:

- Putty with glass.
- Shoes and shoe polish.
- Bookkeeping and help with tax returns.
- Management consultancy and training.

If you are providing the bacon, can you also offer the egg? If it does not suit your production set-up, can you buy in the egg and sell it on at a profit?

Alternatively, if you are providing a service for which an add-on service is indicated and which you cannot provide, can you sub-contract it or otherwise work in co-operation with someone else?

## Ask the customer

The bacon to go with your egg may not be obvious, but a good way to spot it is to ask your customer.

'How do you use this chemical Mr Smith? You mix it with oil? – we can supply the oil!'

Better still, in this situation, would be to be able to tell the customer that you can sell him the two products already mixed.

### SUMMARY OF KEY POINTS

1.  Look at things from the customer's angle. How does your company and its products appear to him? What does he want which you can give him to improve his perception of you and increase your sales to him?

2.  Find out exactly how your customer uses your product and what else he uses.

3.  Invite your customer to visit *you*. Show him round, invite his ideas and show that you care about serving him well.

4.  Seek out 'bacon and egg' possibilities. Can *you* provide something he buys from someone else – something which is used with your product?

# CHAPTER 12

# LONG-TERM THINKING

## What does the market want?

Standing back from the day-to-day struggle to take a long-term view of the business is essential – and especially so in the matter of where your revenue will come from and how it will be generated in future. A policy is needed to provide direction and a plan of action based on it to achieve whatever profit objectives you have set yourself.

One thing is absolutely certain. Your business, to be successful in the medium to long term, *must* be 'market driven'. It is what the market wants that counts – and the market will always be changing. Avoid at all costs the idea that your excellent product or service will always be excellent in the eyes of your customers or potential customers. It may start that way, and your pride in your product may be well and truly justified. Don't allow this pride to make your business a 'product driven' one: ultimately this will be disastrous.

### Selling with the brakes on

A good example of this error was Henry Ford's persistence with the Model T.

This was a first-class product which in time failed to meet the needs of the buying public who were looking for model variations, add-ons and colours other than Ford's famous black.

Ford came close to being put out of business by General Motors, who were prepared to offer various designs to meet the aspirations of the market. Growing affluence and the desire of many car owners to be 'different' had changed the market since the time that Ford developed his policy.

Your policy must be based on the idea of a changing market and allow for it.

## Research and Development

R & D is not a subject for the big companies only. You may not be able to afford vast sums of money for developing new products and services, but some work will be necessary in this direction. Quite frequently a small and relatively inexpensive change to a product can be enough to keep it competitive.

Try the following checklist:

- Is there any cheap and easy change we can make which will keep our product ahead?
  - colour?
  - material used?
  - packaging?
- What are the current trends in the market which may affect our product?
  - disposable products?
  - greater durability?
- What are the competition doing?
  - price?
  - design?

Looking further ahead you should ask:

What is the market likely to want 1 year from now, 2 years, 5 years?

Will your product or service meet these wants?

If not, what new or changed products must be developed?

## Deciding the sales policy

Arguably the most important question to be addressed before defining the policy is: 'What business are we in?' (See Chapter 1.)

Once the question has been properly answered, the next steps in policy formulation can be taken. There will be a number of alternative lines of action open to you depending on the nature of your product or service, the life-cycle of your product (mousetraps go on for years, computers can be obsolete in months), the size and stability of your market and so on.

When looking at some of those alternatives, we will assume that you wish to increase profits. Surely this goes without saying, you may object: don't all businessmen want to increase profits? In fact there are some businesses in which the owners, having reached a satisfactory profit level, do not want to go any further. This in itself can be the sales policy — steady as we go.

However, for those who are looking for profit growth the following are some options:

## 1. Concentrating on high-yielding products or services
We saw in Chapter 1 how some sales can be non-profitable and yet be thought to yield a profit. Analysing the costs associated with each customer, product, service or market can identify those activities which give good results, those which only contribute to fixed costs and those which make a loss.

Having placed the products in such categories you have the option of switching resources to the high yielders and phasing out the rest.

## A danger to avoid

It might be possible to concentrate heavily or exclusively on one line of business and, by so doing, to maximise profit. Beware of placing all your eggs in one basket — especially if a significant percentage of sales is to one major customer.

If the product is vulnerable to being superseded by a competitor's offering, and/or your major customer might stop giving you orders, you could be in the soup.

Some judgement will be required to assess the risk and you could well decide that a spread of business, including some of the less profitable lines, is a wise precaution.

## 2. Concentrating on fast movers
At least one famous business was founded on the old principle of 'Pile 'em high and sell 'em cheap'. This could apply to your business — providing you are prepared to switch fast to a more

upmarket product if and when the market changes. It is better to sell 10 widgets at £1 profit each than 3 at £3 profit each. Analysis of your sales costs and revenue is needed to find out if this principle applies in your case.

### 3. Concentrating on selected places or areas

It normally costs more to sell something in an area where the customers are thin on the ground and a lot of travelling time and cost is involved. Your policy might include a calculated decision to seek business only in selected areas which you can deal with at relatively low cost. This often means areas where customers are close together, enabling a salesperson to visit more in a day and deliveries to be combined on one vehicle/trip.

Such a policy will of course restrict your market to the chosen area and will place a limit on expansion. The limit may be so far ahead that it causes no immediate worry, but if you do want to expand eventually, preparation for it cannot start too soon. One option is to find another area of high customer density and prepare a plan to open a branch in that area. A satellite warehouse, sales office or even a factory may be needed and planning ahead for these is a long-term job.

Of course, another important factor in choosing a preferred area will be the strength or otherwise of the competition there.

### 4. Concentrating on selected types of customers

It might be thought that a small retail shop, a chiropody practice or, say, a typewriter repair service are all businesses in which the opportunity to select customers is virtually non-existent. In fact this is not the case. The advertising used (e.g. in up-market as against down-market magazines), the appearance of the premises and their location, can all influence the type of customers who will contact the business. Prices charged can also have an effect.

## Identify your best market segment

If your business employs a sales force (or perhaps one individual looks after sales), then positive action can be taken. A company selling computer equipment might decide that banks, insurance companies, building societies and others in the financial world are a better bet than, say, light engineering companies. The sales force could concentrate on the chosen area and be trained in the nature of the businesses concerned. Again, an analysis of sales could point you in the right direction. What is the ratio of calls made to sales gained in the various industries you have dealt with? A similar comparison could be made between large and small businesses you sell to.

## Combining the options

A business consultant setting up with a junior partner examined the various factors of area, type of customer, etc. He decided that the best customers would be small to medium-sized companies, which would not be likely to employ in-house specialists but would need specialist advice from time to time.

Market research showed that there were about 2000 such businesses within a 30-mile radius of his home in the Home Counties to the west of London. This gave him a good selling area backed up by the proximity of London itself and the many companies located there. He selected his 'product' carefully and decided to concentrate on productivity and profitability advice as being the greatest perceived needs of the market.

Thus he chose his type of customers, his main products and his area. In addition he decided on a price which was competitive with the big consulting companies on the basis that (a) his overheads were lower and (b) the big boys had largely priced themselves out of the small–medium market.

Some combination of the alternatives will form the medium- to long-term element of a consciously thought-out policy – a far better approach than just taking on any business which happens to come along or knocking on every door.

### 5. Acquisition – another potential way to increase revenue

The classic acquisition success is the one in which Company A buys Company B, takes over all B's customers, sells all B's assets and then satisfies all B's customers from its own original resources. Nice work if you can get it!

In reality this classic result is not easy to achieve. Some of B's

146

customers are likely to move on elsewhere – displeased with the change. Some of B's staff will leave and take customers with them, and if you make people redundant, you are encouraging the process.

In addition you may find when the takeover is completed that the sales levels are not all that you were led to believe. These and other hazards await the would-be purchaser.

However, acquisition is a way to increase revenue. Ideally the company acquired will be one with a good reputation and whose owners will help you in taking over. Just handing you the key and leaving you to it could be damaging, whereas a friendly hand in introducing you to customers well in advance is a great help. This will give you a chance to establish rapport with the customers and to assure them that you will look after them well.

It is also important that the acquired company offers a complete new range of customers in an area which you can adequately handle. If the product or service can be provided more cheaply from the combined companies, e.g. by cutting out the cost of a warehouse, better machine utilisation or a shared accounting service, so much the better. It is not just additional revenue by virtue of more sales which should be sought. Making each sale more profitable as a result of reduced cost per sale is another target.

### 6. Vertical integration

A company making, say, plastic bags for sale to other companies for packaging of their products will probably buy plastic tube in lay-flat roll form. The tube will be cut into the lengths required and the lengths sealed at one end to create the bags.

The manufacturers of the tube will charge a price which includes a profit mark-up and the company making the bags will do likewise. The opportunity for both companies lies in combining so that both slices of revenue and profit are enjoyed by one business.

This vertical integration can be extended further downwards if, say, a third company prints sales slogans, product description etc. on the bags before they are finally sold on.

Any one of these three companies could increase its sales revenue by integration with neighbours in the chain. At the same time some of the other potential benefits of acquisition may be available such as reduced overheads. Another way to look at it is to see a 'downstream' business, if integrated, as a captive market – or at least a captive company.

### 7. Working in co-operation

Not every business has the cash resources to acquire other businesses, whether to obtain new customers or the benefits of vertical integration.

In addition, not all business people want to take such a step. A less dramatic alternative is to find another business – not a competitor – which serves similar customers and with which a co-operative arrangement can increase sales for both. The idea depends on mutual support, trust and recognition that co-operation will increase revenue for both parties. There need be no financial link, although some people work the system on a commission basis. Some real-life examples best illustrate how the system can work.

## Consultants and computers

A management consultant specialised in organisational studies and marketing. He had a working knowledge of computers and computing, but was not an expert in development or application of hardware and software. From time to time his clients' needs and his recommendations had computing elements and implications which were too esoteric for him to handle. He found a competent computer consultant to whom he sub-contracted the computing side of a project; resulting in a complete job and happy clients.

Subsequent discussion between the two consultants quickly revealed opportunities for them both. Each had clients requiring, from time to time, the skills of the other consultant. This, it was realised, virtually doubled the client base for both men and, as experience showed, led to greater earnings for both. All that was necessary was an oral agreement to recommend each other – or sub-contract – in appropriate cases.

## Progress by design

A business requiring advertising hoardings or display material for exhibitions and trade fairs would use a company offering design work. Having obtained the designs and artwork, the company would then use another company to build frameworks, supports, stands and the like on which the display material could be mounted.

Sometimes the frames, supports and so on were constructed first and then a design service would be contracted. This meant that the design company and the construction company were frequently in a position to promote each other's products. By agreeing to do so both businesses increased their earnings.

There are many such opportunities available to businesses willing to commit themselves to a friendly arrangement with another compatible business on a basis of trust and mutual support. A link-up may be possible between:

- Accountants and insurance brokers.
- Various trades in the building industry.
- Printers and designers.
- Specialist engineering companies.

Actively to look for and make use of such opportunities could form part of your sales policy. Action will then result from a positive decision and not be the accidental by-product of, say, a chance discussion.

## 8. Reciprocal business

Is there some other business from which you buy products or services and which could buy from you? If so, a reciprocal sales agreement could suit you both and increase your sales volume. You may buy raw materials from Company A whilst they buy from Company B – your competitor – products which you can supply. A proposal that Company A buy from you in future in exchange for your continuing purchase from them could produce a beneficial result.

If you need supplies from somewhere, why not get them from a potential customer? A positive policy decision to *seek* such opportunities is quite different from passively allowing the odd one to develop by chance – or worse, to allow them to slip by unnoticed.

## A policy which suits the customer

This is another area for long-term thinking. The first requirement is a sales policy which says that the customer needs come first. If we want the orders we must make it easy for the customer to place them. Constantly considering how this can be done is a must and the means may have to change as the business grows, to suit new products or to suit new markets. What may be acceptable to our customers in south-east England may have no appeal to a Frenchman, a Spaniard or a Greek. They may have other ways of doing things which must be respected. They may want prices to be quoted on a delivered basis, i.e. cost, insurance and freight. If you insist on your UK practice of quoting ex-works you are placing a difficulty in the way of the customer, a difficulty which may cause him to give up and look elsewhere.

## EDI – a developing opportunity

Electronic Data Interchange, better known by the initials EDI, is a system by means of which companies can communicate with each other via computer terminals. One of the major areas of EDI development is in the transmission of orders from buyer to seller. No paperwork or personal contact is required, thus reducing cost and time.

However, the system is not just a case of tapping out a message on a keyboard to be read on a computer screen at the other end of the line. Pre-arranged codes are used – for example to describe products – and the coding systems are being developed by industry groups and government agencies on an international basis. The need to participate in EDI is growing all the time, with some major companies already only willing to do business with others on the system. EDI makes doing business easier, including dealing with Customs and Excise in exporting, importing and VAT transactions. It is imperative that if your industry is developing EDI you should, if you have not already done so, find out about it and prepare for it. It is almost certain that one day you will have to use it. Your trade association, your bank or the Department of Trade and Industry should be able to advise you on developments which will affect you.

### Don't let EDI scare you

The prospect of EDI may sound daunting. Don't be dismayed at the idea. It is not all that hard to understand or to implement — nor need it be very expensive.

On the plus side it will offer the chance of reduced clerical costs, will speed up transactions (including getting paid!) and make your business more accessible to customers.

## Franchising — expansion without capital

Successful small to medium-sized businesses can often find themselves in a situation where expansion is inhibited by lack of capital. It may be clear to the owners of the business that there would be greater opportunities for the product or service if only the cash were available to penetrate new markets and provide the product.

A way to raise the capital is to franchise your business. The principle is a simple one. In exchange for a fee, a royalty on sales or both you allow the franchisee to operate a 'branch' of your business. The franchisee provides the funds for his operation, thus solving your problem of lack of capital for expansion.

However, this is a longer-term idea as there is a lot of detail to be worked on.

### What you must offer

In addition to a genuinely promising product you will have to offer a fair and reasonable deal which is legally sound and also give your franchisees some support.

This, depending on your product, could include:

- Finding suitable premises.
- Advertising and other forms of promotion.
- Training and ongoing advice.
- Product development back-up.

### Picking the right franchisee

It is not enough for the franchisee to have the money — he must have the ability and determination to make his franchise succeed.

If not, you will earn little or nothing on royalties (or on supplies you would otherwise sell him) and the reputation of your product could suffer.

The aspiring former docker with a large redundancy cheque may not be the right person to run a business demanding clerical skills or, say, experience of dealing with the public.

The early retired bank manager may not be the person best suited to running a franchised fast food outlet or a business requiring manual skills.

Notwithstanding these limitations and demands on your time and skills, franchising your business is a way to achieve expansion and increase profits. You will have the advantage that your franchisees will be working for themselves — not on your payroll — and they will have a powerful motivation to make a go of it. They are likely to work longer and harder than a salaried employee to obtain a return on their investment.

This offers you additional security and the prospect of greater profit.

## SUMMARY OF KEY POINTS

1.     Increasing revenue should be viewed and planned on a long-term basis. Short term action can be useful but should not be a recurrent substitute for a longer view.

      Don't neglect research and development. Your product or service will have to change in some way some time.

2.     The essential basis for future action is the market, and your business should be 'market driven' not 'product driven'.

3.     A sales policy should be carefully worked out and the various alternatives considered.

      You could concentrate for example:

- On high-yielding products and services
- On fast movers — even if low in unit profit yield
- On particular places or areas
- On selected types of customer

or you can combine some of these alternatives.

4.  Acquisition can be a means to widen your range of customers and so increase revenue. You can also consider vertical integration, reciprocal business arrangements, direct marketing or some form of co-operation with another compatible company.

5.  Find ways to make it easy for people to buy your product in the longer term. Include EDI in your study.

6.  Examine franchising as a way to expand and increase profits. This is a means to 'raise capital' with a reduced risk.

# CHAPTER · 13

# *INCREASING PRODUCTIVITY*

If, as a result of some effective long- and short-term thinking, you have increased demand for your product or service, can you meet the demand? Are you in any case making optimum use of your resources and enjoying the lowest possible unit production costs?

Whatever the situation, maximising productivity – that is, getting the best possible output from your resources – is essential to the long-term health of your business and to profits. This means intelligent and effective use of your physical assets such as machinery and premises and of your most important resource – your people.

Obtaining the best results depends on two basic needs:

1. Effective organisation and control; and
2. Motivated people.

The subject of your people, their commitment and enthusiasm for the job, is covered in Chapter 14.

## Effective organisation and control

Consider a company making lawnmowers.

There will be an array of different departments, each contributing to the final product and its delivery to the customer. There will be:

- Purchasing – obtaining castings, sheet metal, nuts and bolts, etc.
- Various machining functions – making wheels, blades and other parts.

- Assembly – putting all the bits together.
- Testing.
- Packing.
- Despatch.

Somewhere in all this will be a stores function, quality control, paint spraying and possibly other operations.

Each of these areas of activity can be viewed in isolation, but this will not show the true picture. The productivity of the whole organisation will be governed by the interrelations of the various functions, and the least effective of them will dominate the rest. If, for example, the section making wheels can only produce 100 per day (enough for 50 lawnmowers) then there is no point in the blade making department producing enough blades for 200 lawnmowers – unless the work is deliberately organised in such a way that, having stockpiled blades, the same production resources are used to make other parts.

If the wheels section slips up and produces 100 faulty wheels, then all the subsequent processes will be adversely affected by a shortage of wheels.

Some form of control and organisation is needed to ensure that:

1.  Each part of the whole has a clear role with established targets and standards which are mutually compatible; and

2.  If and when any part of the organisation fails to maintain output at the required level, corrective action is promptly taken. This implies a monitoring function in order to spot any deviation from the plan of work.

Without such provisions achievement of the full production potential will be a hit-and-miss process – often with more miss than hit. Let us look at some examples.


## A typical organisational anomaly

Imagine an office in a mail order company. Orders arrive by post with cheques for payment. Each order needs to be checked, sorted and allocated to a despatch section. It is not untypical in such cases to find that staff are allocated to jobs like this:

|  | No. of staff | Capacity per day |
|---|---|---|
| Order checking | 1 clerk | 200 |
| Order sorting | 1 clerk | 400 |
| Allocation | 1 clerk | 300 |
| Despatch | 3 clerks | 150 |

Such an arrangement means that despatch is a bottleneck and whatever the other clerks do the maximum output is 150 orders per day.

If the allocation clerk is moved to the despatch department and his or her work done by the sorting clerk, then output would rise to 200 per day. The sorting clerk, now doing allocation as well, has sufficient capacity to handle the additional work.

It might be argued that in this simple example the organisational weakness was obvious. This is true – once the weakness is pointed out. In real life such imbalances are only too common and often disguised by the application of Parkinson's Law. The underemployed people will spread their work out to fill the time available and the situation is only likely to be revealed if some work study is carried out.

## Machinery out of balance

It is not only people and their output capacity that can be poorly organised. Situations occur in which, say, machine A, with a capacity of 100 items per hour, is fed with output from machine B with a capacity of 50 items per hour.

Mixing manual operations with machines can also result in lost production. In a real-life case an item of furniture was being made. The early stages of manufacture were mechanised and output was high. The assembly stage was purely manual and involved fixing timbers together using a hammer and nails. The latter process was slow and required two operators to keep up with the mechanised process. By the simple expedient of bringing in a compressed air gun to replace hammers the output of the assembly stage was more than doubled. This saved labour and, with a suitable re-arrangement of jobs and machines, output was increased by 100%. Costs − including depreciation on the machinery − increased by only about 10%, yielding a significant increase in profits.

These examples point to the need to spend some time analysing the various operations.

## Analysing − what to look for

A routine check should aim to establish:

- What exactly is being done.
- The sequence of operations.
- Volumes of work.
- Flexibility (or otherwise) of labour.
- Human and machine capacities.
- The means used to co-ordinate activities − if any.
- The work scheduling method − if any.
- What happens during periods of machine down times (e.g. for maintenance), employee sickness or other emergencies.
- Opportunities to replace human effort with machines, releasing the people for non-repetitive work.
    Perhaps you could then apply the Japanese technique: having found a machine which will replace one of two people − buy *two* machines and continue to employ both people.

Look, in particular, for the following symptoms which can point to opportunities:

- Labour intensive operations − can they be economically mechanised?
- Manual and machine operations mixed in the production sequence − are they compatible?
- Piles of semi-finished products waiting for machine or labour availability − is there an imbalance or lack of control?
- Idle machinery − why?
- People doing an inordinate amount of 'tidying up', cleaning or maintaining equipment. This could indicate underemployed people who are finding 'work' to fill the day.
- Frequent panics and ad hoc changes to work schedules, e.g.

157

switching from one type of work or product to another. This suggests lack of forward planning and control.

Switching jobs in mid-stream almost invariably loses output as a result of increased set-up times and general disruption. In office work it often means time lost when staff have to re-focus their thinking on to the new task — and then back again to the interrupted task.

- Finished product, semi-finished product or paperwork criss-crossing factory floors or moving from one place to another and then back again.
- Product or paperwork which requires, say, 1 hour's work but takes, say, an elapsed time of 10 hours to be disposed of.

In one dramatic real-life case paperwork going into an office was taking up to 120 days to re-emerge. The actual time required for each job was about 6 *hours*. The rest of the time the documents were lying around in piles, waiting for spurious checking and generally stuck in an unorganised process which was not monitored in any way. The speed with which a job was cleared was largely determined by reaction to angry clients.

- Lack of reliable information as to quantities of semi-finished or finished products in stock, backlogs, capacities and/or the whereabouts of paperwork or materials.

An interesting and illustrative comment made by a director of Davy Morris the crane manufacturers was reported in the *Financial Times* (11 July 1990). Talking about the problems that the company had tackled, he was quoted as saying: 'There was a lot of stock and work in progress in the factory. They (the managers) had no accurate information. The data had decomposed. In short, there was no system underpinning what they did. They didn't know in which direction to move.'

## After the analysis — what then?

The first requirement is to ensure that the organisational structure is right and that everyone is aware of it. A clear organisation chart should be drawn up showing who is in charge of what and who does what. Every member of staff should have a copy — nothing in it should be regarded as confidential or secret.

Drawing up the chart will pinpoint any areas where authority and responsibility have been blurred. The chart should make these aspects of the business abundantly clear. Nothing very complex is required – something along the lines of the chart shown in Figure 9 will suffice. Such a chart shows who calls the shots and the broad areas of responsibility.

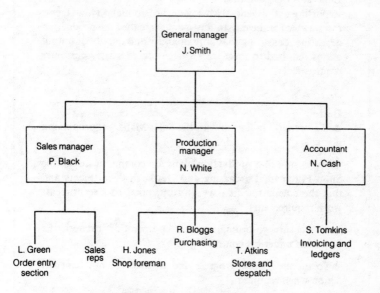

Figure 9. A basic organisation chart.

The organisation chart should be supported by a job description for *every* employee, giving more detail of what they are expected to do. For example the job description for N. White, the production manager in Figure 9, might be as shown on page 160.

The result of producing the organisation chart and the job descriptions is to remove any uncertainty as to who carries which can and reduce the chance that something will not be done which should be done. Duplication of work should also be avoided.

## Getting the flow right

The analysis will have revealed any time-wasting movement of paper or product and identified the most effective sequencing of

159

**Job description:** PRODUCTION MANAGER

**General responsibilities:**
Reporting to the General Manager, the Production Manager is responsible for the day-to-day management of the production department ensuring that both quantity and quality of output are as required to meet sales forecasts and satisfy customer requirements.

**Duties:**
- To prepare, in liaison with the Sales Manager, production plans.

- To ensure that production plans are communicated to the Shop Foreman, Purchasing and Despatch departments and that these departments have, in turn, plans to meet forecast work requirements.

- To ensure co-ordination and co-operation between the functions under his control.

- To monitor work progress and to take prompt remedial action when required.

- To maintain a quality control system and to ensure that quality standards are maintained.

- To see that despatch information is passed promptly to the Accounts department with full information for invoicing purposes.

- To report, weekly, to the General Manager, levels of output and costs.

- To maintain, as required, a training programme for staff in his department and to ensure that adequate plans exist for succession and absence cover.

- To maintain a planned maintenance schedule for machinery and equipment.

etc.

work. Bottlenecks and under-used resources should have been spotted.

With the involvement of the various heads of department a work flow chart can now be drawn up to show the sequence of operations required to produce the best result. The type of chart shown in Figure 7 can be used and examination of it will reveal whether all unnecessary movement – or illogical movement – has been eliminated.

### Be sure to tell them

Every member of staff should have a copy of the flow chart. If people are not told what is required to be done they cannot be expected to do it.

## Flexibility

Some people fear that if an employee is given a job description he or she will refuse to do any job which is not clearly described in it. This is rarely the case in practice – in fact it is more likely that jobs will get done with job descriptions than without. The responsibilities and duties can be described in fairly general terms and it should be made clear that they are a *guide*, not a list of laws.

This is important in maintaining labour flexibility, especially in the smaller company where it is often necessary for people to switch from one job to another. This requirement can be built in to the job description.

## Nothing should be permanent

Flexibility must also be maintained in another sense. The organisation chart, flow chart and job description should all be regarded as temporary. Nothing should be treated as carved on tablets of stone. Circumstances will change both internally and externally and the company must be ready to change with it.

Growth, for example, may require the sales department to split into two regional teams each with a regional manager. A new product may best be handled by appointing a second production foreman. Both of these changes will mean a new organisation chart and some repositioning of duties.

The introduction of a new machine or the discovery of an opportunity to improve efficiency may necessitate a change to work flow – and possibly a job description change too.

## Create a management team

Once the work methods and who does what questions are sorted out it is vital that a means exists to ensure that things do not drift apart again.

To a great extent this is the responsibility of the person in charge (the General Manager in Figure 9). However, no one should be so unwise as to assume that he or she alone can make all the decisions or can be aware, at all times, of everything that is going on. A smoothly running operation depends on the involvement of many people and at least the various department heads. The people must work as a team.

### Consult, consult

This means that they must be consulted by the boss and consult each other. They must not regard their own departments as separate entities but as part of a whole. This means that each department must be aware of the needs and purposes of other departments and what they must do to work effectively together. This in turn demands effective and *continuous* communication.

### Meet to plan

Regular planning meetings – working to a strict agenda – will normally meet the need. Much will depend on the boss, who must run the meetings skilfully and make sure that they are creative and constructive. Griping sessions and idle chatter get you nowhere.

### What should the team do?

The team should be made aware of the objectives of the company as a whole and the consequent objectives for their own parts of it.

Ideally, each team member will have been involved in the objective-setting process in the first place.

With this knowledge the team can perform the following functions:

● *Co-ordinate activities*
Setting or re-setting of priorities, changes to schedules and general progress chasing are typical topics for the team to work on.

If the sales manager is receiving feedback from the market indicating a reducing demand for plastic widgets but an increase in demand for steel widgets, this could have an impact on everyone. Production may have to switch emphasis to steel widgets with implications for the purchasing section. Stock levels of plastic widgets may need to be re-checked and so on.

● *Deal with the unexpected*
A sudden large order for a hitherto slow-moving product could mean changes all round. The breakdown of a machine could mean a damage limitation exercise such as buying in product, sub-contracting or some fast footwork from the sales team.

Such situations require team effort with a willingness for each part of the company to support the others. The familiar cry of 'That's your problem, mate' has no place in the company which has aspirations to be truly profitable.

● *Exploit opportunities*
Opportunities large and small crop up from time to time. The co-operation of team members is required to exploit them. This could involve transferring an employee from one department to another, modifying a product to meet a customer's needs or even something as basic as re-organising the holiday rota.

● *Control events*
Teamwork reduces the need for and effect of expediency action. Work can be *planned* and monitored more effectively when watertight compartments are eliminated. Work can be better synchronised to make best use of the agreed work flow pattern.

- *Reduce costs*

  Quite frequently the costs incurred in one department are influenced by the actions of another. The classic case is the tension between sales and production. Sales want to please customers asking for small quantities whilst production want long runs to hold down unit production costs.

  Teamwork is needed to reach compromise solutions which keep down costs while not losing marketing opportunities. Give and take may be required to find the optimum *company orientated* solution when the parochial needs of departments are in conflict. If any one function is allowed to dominate another it is likely that costs in the subordinate function will rise.

- *Long-term planning*

  Teams, aware of and understanding the functions of all the team members, can be a powerful aid to long-term corporate planning. The combined knowledge of production, sales, accounting and administrative people is far more likely to result in a successful corporate plan than, say, one dreamed up by the managing director working in isolation. A team developed plan is also more likely to succeed as a result of increased commitment to it by the team members. Even poorly constructed plans can be made to work if the people back them.

## SUMMARY OF KEY POINTS

1. Productivity and its implications for profit depends on effective organisation and control of resources.

2. Check that there are no organisational anomalies which will waste the capacity of people or machines.

3. Carry out an analysis to check what is being done, in what sequence and the volumes of work involved. Look for the symptoms of wasted opportunities.

4. Use an organisation chart and job description to reduce uncertainties and possible duplication of effort.

5.   Examine work flow and produce a work flow chart as a guide to managers and staff.

6.   Create a management *team* and get everyone working as a team. Ensure that you and everyone else knows what teamwork is and how a team works.

CHAPTER · **14**

# *INCREASING THE EFFECTIVENESS OF INDIVIDUALS*

## People are your most important resource

Ideally, all your people and not just your heads of departments will work as a team. This is easy to say, but not so easy to achieve. First of all you need to identify what team work actually is. The easiest way to describe it is to list its characteristics. You can then see whether your business activities exhibit those features and, if not, the areas of improvement open to you.

## The characteristics of a team

1. **A sense of shared purpose**
   All team members are aware of and support objectives to be achieved and the standards of performance laid down.

2. **A sense of group pride**
   'We are the champions' chant the football fans. Sad though it is that this *esprit de corps* is so often misapplied, any team does need a sense of pride.
   This pride should not be confused with complacency. It is one thing to be pleased that the group is of champion status — quite another to believe the group will always be champions. Pride in performance must be mixed with pride in the forward thinking of the group and its awareness of threats to it.

166

3. **The team works as a single organism**

   Each part depends on each other part. This interdependence is recognised, fostered and is never resented.

Boiled down to everyday terms the members of a team will:

- Always find support when needed from other team members.
- Willingly join in dealing with an emergency.
- Regard group problems as their own problems.
- Be pleased with the successes of other team members.
- Depend on each other to do what has been promised.
- Enjoy working with other team members.
- Pick up jobs to be done without having to be asked.
- Know what is going on and why.
- Be frank with each other − in a constructive way.
- Talk a common language.
- Feel that they matter and 'belong'.

Achieving this state of affairs will not come about by accident. Teams have to be created and nurtured. This is the role of the team leader, and it is on him or her that the profitable use of human resources will depend.


## The team leader's job

The successful team leader will first of all have a clear idea as to what is to be achieved. Required output levels, revenues to be achieved and quality standards need to be laid down and communicated to the team members. With the participation of the members a plan will be drawn up to achieve the desired results.

The team leader should then:

- Learn as much as possible about each of the individuals for whom he is responsible. Strengths, weaknesses, likes and dislikes should all be taken into account along with the personality features of each person. This knowledge assists in knowing how best to use each person and the degree of supervision and support necessary.
- Brief individuals and the team as a whole about objectives, priorities and opportunities.
- Set clear standards and deadlines for work to be done.
- Organise his own time in order to be available to team

members for guidance, discussion and decision-making.

- Ensure that workloads are fairly distributed between team members and that members are encouraged to support each other.
- Brief the team on progress, any changes of circumstances and any information relevant to the team members and their jobs. In particular, any successes should be communicated – with a 'thank you' to those concerned.

Whilst these actions will encourage a team attitude the needs of the individuals must not be neglected. The effective team leader will also:

- Allow time to explain fully to each individual what is expected of him and why.
- Listen sympathetically to the problems of individuals and provide help to overcome difficulties.
- Give greater responsibility, opportunity and challenge to individuals who seek for and would benefit from them. Remember – delegation, properly done, motivates.
- Praise where praise is due. Such recognition is most effective when made public.
- Keep promises made to individuals.
- Encourage individuals to come up with ideas – and see that those ideas are given a full and sympathetic hearing.

    It was a very poor team leader who said, when asked if he encouraged ideas, 'Yes, if anyone has a suggestion I always hear it out before I reject it.' No doubt he intended to express himself differently, but the words he used reflected the reality of his approach.

These actions will help to motivate the individuals and make them feel that while the team is important they are important too. No one, however junior, should be left out – profits depend on the good work of everyone and not just the top layers.


## Other ways to maximise individual potential

The team will only be as strong as the sum of its parts and a weak member can place a burden on the shoulders of the others. Every individual needs to be helped and encouraged to reach maximum effectiveness. This can involve a number of actions on the part of management, starting with the right approach to recruitment and continuing with skilful induction and on-going training: all of which amounts to a productive management style.

## Getting the right people for the job

Recruitment is an expensive and time-consuming activity, and a disciplined procedure must be followed to avoid costly errors.

The minimum recruitment requirements are as follows:

- To prepare a job description for the position to be filled.

- To construct a 'person profile' based on the job description. If the job description includes contact with customers either face to face or on the telephone then there will be a requirement for:

  - Courtesy and patience.
  - Pleasant speaking voice.
  - Calmness under fire.

If meeting customers face to face is involved, then appearance becomes important and you might also want to add a degree of experience of customer contact to your list.

Other possibilities might include:

  - Keyboard skills.
  - Languages.
  - Knowledge of export documentation.
  - Willingness to work unsocial hours.
  - Letter-writing skills.
  - Basic mathematics.
  - Physical strength.

Whatever the needs it is worth taking the trouble to work out the profile, rather than working from what is often a rather vague and general idea of what is wanted.

- To search, perhaps by advertising, for someone who fits the profile.

  The profile should be used as a basis for the advertisement, which should be specific about the job (from the job description) and the type of person required.

The job will be briefly described in terms such as clerical work, use of telephone, operating fax machines, meeting clients. General descriptions such as 'Interesting office work' or 'Challenging position' should be avoided. If the advertisement is specific and precise it will enable job-seekers to judge whether it is worth applying and save you a lot of wasted time.

The advertisement should mention the main requirements arising from the person profile. For instance, it might say: 'Knowledge of export documentation, ability to work under pressure and accurately to carry out calculation of freight and insurance rates.' An imprecise person description such as 'Keen, ambitious and willing to learn' could fit many people who would not be right for the job.

An alternative to advertising is to give the job description and profile to existing members of the team and ask them if they know of anyone suitable. The advantages in this method lie in the fact that existing staff will have an understanding of the work and the skills needed and will not be likely to introduce someone who is unsuitable.

Don't go for high fliers − unless you really need them.

It is a common mistake to look for highly qualified people with ambition when the job does not require these features. The idea that a routine clerical job will be better done by an 18-year-old with four 'A' levels is a mistake. Such people quickly become bored with routine, undemanding work and will move on.

- To interview methodically and objectively.

Prejudices ('I don't like people with posh accents') should be set aside for starters. We all have prejudices and they take many forms. They have no place in intelligent interviewing.

The purpose of the interview is to see how closely the applicant matches the person profile. This can be achieved by encouraging the applicant to talk. The interviewer should ask questions (in a friendly manner) and listen, listen, listen.

## You have the person − what then?

There is a marked tendency for people to leave jobs in the first six months. The early losses are often due to poor induction of the new employee, who will be strongly influenced by his or her treatment in the first few weeks – and especially in the first few days.

Every new employee should be treated as a VIP – which is what they are. You need them and need them to be motivated – after all you will have spent time and money to find them and now you want some return for your investment and the salary you are paying. The result depends at least as much on you as the employee.

Here is a checklist of basic induction action:

- Welcome the new employee on the first day – make an effort and tell the newcomer how pleased you are to see him.
- Make sure that all the other employees, including your receptionist, know about the newcomer and what his job will be.
- Have everything ready such as desk, equipment, stationery or whatever is needed to do the job – all clean and tidy and in working order.
- Arrange for someone to help the newcomer over the first few days. Introduction to colleagues, what to do about lunch and even where to find the lavatories are all important.
- Have some work ready. Spending two or three days doing nothing can be devastating to morale and confidence and a sensible programme of work is vital.

Induction does not, however, suddenly end after the first few days. Follow-up, involving progress sessions with the boss, is most valuable and encourages enthusiasm. Problems can be sorted out before they become serious obstacles – for example the need for some training might need to be identified.

## Training – an investment for future profits

Often neglected, training is an essential ingredient to a profitable operation. Technical and managerial skills are the bedrock of high productivity and high-quality work.

Training should be an on-going process with tailor-made plans for every employee. Techniques such as On-Job-Training should be used (this is *not* the same as 'sitting next to Nellie'), as well as more formal training methods either in-house or at outside seminars and courses. All this need not be horrifyingly expensive and when methodically carried out has a value many times its cost.

Among the topics which everyone should be taught – in

addition to the technical skills required by their jobs – are:

● *Time management*
As much as 30% of an employee's time can be wasted if he does not know how to manage it.

Most of the essentials of good time management can be taught in two to three hours and the pay-off can be substantial. Make your people, at all levels, aware of the things which waste time so that they can do something about it. Time-wasters include:

- Boss not available to make decisions.
- Badly designed paperwork.
- Unscheduled meetings and other interruptions.
- Lack of or unclear instructions.
- Skipping from one job to another.
- Failure to delegate or to delegate properly.
- Lack of a system.
- Lack of personal priorities and working plan.

Much of the time lost for reasons such as these will diminish as soon as the cause is pointed out.

● *Delegation*
How to delegate is not a skill that people are born with. It needs to be taught. Delegation offers benefits to the delegator, the delegatee and the company. The benefits include reduced pressure on the boss, greater job interest for the delegatee, better absence cover and higher productivity.

But to achieve the benefits people need to know how to overcome obstacles expressed like this:

1.  'I can do it myself more quickly.' This is probably true and if you want to go on doing it yourself for ever then forget about delegation.

2.  'I have no one suitable to pass the work on to.' Why not? Have you recruited the wrong people or failed to train them?

3.  'My staff are already overloaded.' Are they? Ask them – you may get a surprising answer.

● *Social skills*
How well does your telephonist deal with people?
Is your shop foreman abusive to delivery drivers?

How does your accounts clerk go about chasing debts? Constructively or like an angry rottweiler?

Skills in dealing with people, both inside and outside the business, can make the difference between getting things done well and not getting them done at all.

- *Communication skills*
  Effective use of the telephone both to make and receive calls is important. The simple failure to take a message properly can result in an order improperly handled or even lost altogether.

  The ability to write letters is another skill which encourages new orders, payment of bills and other contributions to profit. The misuse of terms such as 'its' and 'it's' can make your business look amateurish. Sometimes businessmen make themselves look silly – as in the case of the insurance company employee who wrote: 'We will take statements from the deceased relatives.'

  Similarly, letters written in a style more suitable to Charles Dickens's lawyer not only make you look pompous but are also difficult to understand. A real-life letter included the sentence: 'We wait, dear sirs, your advices with anticipation of a favourable outcome to the above captioned matter.' This was written by a law graduate and demonstrated that the inability to write understandable English is not limited to those with little education.

## Apart from training – what else?

There is a particular style of management which encourages hard work and good work. The characteristics of the well-managed operation – as far as people are concerned – are:

- Employees are never inhibited in talking to superiors and discussing work with them. Bad news and mistakes made will be communicated to the boss without fear.
- The boss frequently involves employees in problem-solving and decision-taking. Employees' ideas are actively sought when setting objectives.
- Staff are never 'motivated' by fear or punishment – always by reward linked to the achievement of agreed objectives.

- Staff at all levels feel responsible for achieving the goals of the company.
- There is continuous communication in all directions regarding goals to be achieved (and why) and information on progress, problems, etc.
- Information received by employees is accepted and openly discussed. Employees do not view information passed to them with suspicion.
- Any upward flow of information is freely given, honest, complete and accurate.
- Seniors are well aware of the problems of subordinates and understand them.
- Problems are shared.
- Decision-making occurs at all levels, not just at the top.
- Controls, e.g. on quality and timing, are delegated to all levels with some activities mainly controlled at the lower levels.
- Performance results are used for guidance and encouragement – never to punish.

Achieving this situation is not easy and may require a substantial change in your management style. The effort will be well repaid in improved output and work quality – and ultimately in profits.

## What about money?

A fair and reasonable rate for the job is necessary to avoid demotivating the employee. Paying heavily over the odds has little effect except to keep the person with you even if he or she positively hates the job. Paying too little, i.e. less than the market rate or poorly by comparison with colleagues doing a similar job, has a negative effect and this at least must be avoided.

There is no point in reducing profits by paying too much – especially when the employee is seeking satisfaction from more responsibility, improved status or working conditions or clear prospects of advancement. Money is not a substitute for these needs.

## SUMMARY OF KEY POINTS

1. Learn what the effective team leader must do to improve performance (and profits) and work hard at implementation.

2. Get the most out of individuals by effective recruitment, skilful induction and sound training. Find out what 'techniques' are needed to do this.

3. Apply the management style which gets results and pay your people a fair, but not excessive, rate for the job.

# SOURCES OF FURTHER INFORMATION

## Analysing the business

Some easy-to-use mathematical techniques which may help to clarify opportunities for improvement are provided in *Ideas for Enterprising Managers* by Matthew Archer (Mercury Business Books).

The first chapter of this book also suggests ways to give your business (or department) a quick checkover and subsequent chapters deal with other aspects of effectiveness and efficiency.

## Financial aspects

The problem of outstanding debts – how to prevent them and how to collect the cash – is dealt with in *How to Collect the Money you are Owed* by Malcolm Bird (Piatkus Books).

If you are looking for a more general explanation of the financial aspects of business there are some excellent short videos available from Video Arts Ltd, including 'The Balance Sheet Barrier'. This video deals with Capital, Cash-Flow, Gearing, Asset Valuation and other financial topics. Video Arts can be contacted at 68 Oxford Street, London W1N 9LA.

## Purchasing

The importance of buying quality products is stressed by John Kelly in *Purchasing for Profit* (Pitman), one of the titles in the NatWest Small Business series. The pros and cons of bulk buying, estimating quantities and selecting new suppliers are among the other topics covered in this useful book.

## Marketing

Longman Training, Cullum House, North Orbital Road, Denham, Uxbridge, Middlesex UB9 5HL provide a useful self-study pack on how to prepare marketing plans. The pack includes audio cassettes and videos. A glance through the Longman Training catalogue may reveal other packs or videos which would be helpful – there is a particularly strong list of sales technique material.

A stimulating book is *Marketing Ideas for the Small Business* by P. W. and P. F. Sterrett (Mercury Business Books). It provides 46 suggestions for promoting your business plus some advice on advertising.

Also worth reading is *How to Win Customers and Keep Them for Life* by James B. Patterson (Piatkus Books). This book offers advice on making it easy to buy and on 'buying signals', dealing with obstacles and just about everything else in sales technique.

## The people

Two Longman Training videos are well worth looking at: 'Time to Think' deals with time management and includes aspects of teamwork and delegation; 'The Successful Supervisor' adds more to the subject of teams – in particular on team building.

Time management is effectively covered in *The Complete Time Management System* by Godefray and Clark (Piatkus Books). This is probably the most complete treatment of the subject ever written and includes everything from delegation to handling appointments.

Recruiting *and keeping* the most suitable people for the job is explained in *The Best Person for the Job* by Malcolm Bird (Piatkus Books). A section on how to go about delegation will help the reader who is unfamiliar with the full technique.

An older book which is worth seeking out is *The Human Organisation* by Rensis Likert (McGraw-Hill). This is a classic work on the subject of people and their reaction to styles of leadership. Although it was published in 1967, Likert's observations still hold good. The book may be a little academic for some people's taste, but is required reading for serious students of management.

# INDEX

# Business Books for Successful Managers

PIATKUS BUSINESS BOOKS have been created for people like you, busy executives and managers who need expert knowledge readily available in a clear and easy-to-follow format. All the books are written by specialists in their field. They will help you improve your skills quickly and effortlessly in the workplace and on a personal level.

Each book is packed with ideas and good advice which can be put into practice immediately. Titles include:

**The Art of the Hard Sell** *Subtle high pressure tactics that really work*
Robert L. Shook

**The Best Person for the Job** *Where to find them and how to keep them*
Malcolm Bird

**Beware the Naked Man Who Offers You His Shirt** *Do what you love, love what you do and deliver more than you promise* Harvey Mackay

**Brain Power** *The 12-week mental training programme*
Marilyn vos Savant and Leonore Fleischer

**The Complete Book of Business Etiquette**
Lynne Brennan and David Block

**Confident Decision Making** *How to make the right decision every time*
J. Edward Russo and Paul J. H. Schoemaker

**The Complete Time Management System** Christian H.Godefroy

**Dealing with Difficult People** *How to improve your communication skills in the workplace* Roberta Cava

**The Energy Factor** *How to motivate your workforce* Art McNeil

**How to Become Rich and Successful** *A 14-point plan for Business Success*
Charles Templeton

**How to Close Every Sale** Joe Girard with Robert L. Shook

**How to Collect the Money You Are Owed** *Improve your cash flow and increase your profit* Malcolm Bird

**How to Develop and Profit from Your Creative Powers** *Simple techniques for creating new ideas* Michael LeBoeuf

**How to Succeed in Network Marketing** Leonard Hawkins

**How to Win Customers and Keep Them for Life**   Michael LeBoeuf

**Improve Your Profits** *Practical advice for the small- to medium-sized business*   Malcolm Bird

**The Influential Woman** *How to achieve success without losing your femininity*   Lee Bryce

**Leadership Skills for Every Manager** *New techniques to improve organisational effectiveness*   Jim Clemmer and Art McNeil

**Mentoring and Networking** *A woman's guide*   Dr Lily Segerman-Peck

**Marketing Yourself** *How to sell yourself and get the jobs you've always wanted*   Dorothy Leeds

**Organise Yourself**   Ronni Eisenberg with Kate Kelly

**Powerspeak** *The complete guide to public speaking and communication* Dorothy Leeds

**The PowerTalk System** *How to communicate effectively* Christian H. Godefroy and Stephanie Barrat

**Selling by Direct Mail** *An entrepreneurial guide to direct marketing* John W. Graham and Susan K. Jones

**Status** *What it is and how to achieve it*   Philippa Davies

**The Strategy of Meetings**   George David Kieffer

**Telephone Selling Techniques that Really Work** *How to find new business by phone*   Bill Good

**Your Memory** *How it works and how to improve it*   Kenneth L. Higbee

**Your Total Image** *How to communicate success*   Philippa Davies

You too can benefit from expert advice. Just look out for our distinctive Piatkus silver business book jackets in the shops. For a free brochure with further information on our complete range of business titles, please write to:

Business Books Department
Piatkus Books
5 Windmill Street
London, W1P 1HF

PIATKUS

## HOW TO COLLECT THE MONEY YOU ARE OWED
### by Malcolm Bird

Getting paid on time is vital for any business. In *How to Collect the Money You are Owed*, Malcolm Bird gives practical advice on how to organise your invoicing and money collecting systems, improve your cash flow and increase your profitability.

- Learn how to control your cash flow cycle
- Develop an efficient invoicing system
- Get to know your clients and how they operate
- Learn how to chase up money effectively
- Discover what to do if all else fails

*How to Collect the Money You are Owed* will help you save time and money. It is an essential handbook for every office.

Malcolm Bird is the Development Director of an international insurance company.


## HOW TO DEVELOP AND PROFIT FROM YOUR CREATIVE POWERS
### by Michael LeBoeuf

People who know how to create good ideas and turn them into reality will always do well, whatever the future may bring.

- Learn how to get in touch with your creative self
- Strengthen your imagination with 9 simple exercises
- Focus your creative energies on goals that work for you
- Break out of habitual thinking patterns
- Learn simple techniques for creating new ideas at will
- Discover how to present your ideas to other people and turn them into a profitable reality

Michael LeBoeuf PhD is professor of management, organisational behaviour and communications at the University of New Orleans.

## HOW TO CLOSE EVERY SALE
### by Joe Girard

*How To Close Every Sale* includes the fundamental principles, the philosophy, the inside tips and the special factors that have made Joe Girard into the greatest salesman in the world. Let Joe Girard teach you:

- What to say to the procrastinator who wants to 'think it over'
- How to overcome the objection: 'I want to shop around'
- How to make a prospect feel 'obligated' to buy your product
- How to recognise the right time for subtle high-pressure tactics
- How to go double or nothing — and close that sale now or never!

Whilst a salesman with a Chevrolet agency in Detroit, Joe Girard sold over 13,000 cars, a record that put him in *The Guinness Book of World Records* for twelve consecutive years as 'the world's greatest salesman'.

## CONFIDENT DECISION MAKING
### by J. Edward Russo and Paul J.H. Schoemaker

This is the decision-making programme that executives have been waiting for. Buying this book could be among the best decisions you've ever made!

- Avoid the common decision traps of self-taught amateurs
- Learn how to 'frame' a problem correctly
- Recognise and make use of all relevant information
- Follow a scientific decision-making process
- Improve your management skills by making better and more confident decisions

J. Edward Russo is Associate Professor of Marketing and Behavioural Science at Cornell University's Johnson Graduate School of Management and Paul J.J. Schoemaker is Associate Professor of Decision Sciences and Policy in the Graduate School of Business at the University of Chicago.

# THE COMPLETE TIME MANAGEMENT SYSTEM
## by Christian H. Godefroy and John Clark

*The Complete Time Management System* will change the way you work and think. It will increase your enjoyment of life and your chances of success. It will show you:

- How to do in 2 hours what you usually need 4 hours to do
- How to revive your concentration
- How to read 240 pages an hour
- How to make an important decision faster
- How to delegate
- How to organise your office
- How to shorten meetings
- And much, much more

Learn the secrets of time management and you will profit from them all your life.

Christian Godefroy is a training specialist, founder of a publisher company in France and best-selling author.

# LEADERSHIP SKILLS FOR EVERY MANAGER
## by Jim Clemmer and Art McNeil

*Leadership Skills for Every Manager* offers the key to organisational effectiveness. It shows you how to:

- Develop leadership skills throughout your company
- Examine the four leadership elements – vision, values, environment and behaviour – that exist in every organisation
- Build powerful and effective teams
- Align organisational culture
- Train people towards higher personal performance
- Transform good intentions into concrete results

Executives, managers and supervisors will find *Leadership Skills for Every Manager* an invaluable catalyst for action.

Jim Clemmer and Art McNeil are founders and operating executives of The Achieve Group, which specialises in leadership development and organisational effectiveness.

# TELEPHONE SELLING TECHNIQUES THAT REALLY WORK
## How to Find New Business by Phone
### by Bill Good

From first call to final close, Bill Good will help you design a complete, customised telephone prospecting campaign that really works. Learn how to:

- Find new and interested customer and screen out unqualified prospects
- Study your product or service and design an appropriate sales message
- Write winning scripts (over 50 ready-made scripts are included)
- Get more appointments than you ever thought possible
- Fan a flicker of interest into a flame of enthusiasm
- Know when and how to close the sale
- Enjoy your work and increase your sales dramatically

Bill Good is president of Telephone Marketing Inc. in the United States, where his telephone selling techniques have been used successfully to train tens of thousands of salespeople.


# HOW TO WIN CUSTOMERS AND KEEP THEM FOR LIFE
### by Michael LeBoeuf

*How to Win Customers and Keep Them for Life* will be the most important sales aid you will ever have. It will tell you:

- How to provide the best quality customer service
- The reasons which make customers buy and come back
- How to be the kind of person customers like to buy from
- How to find more customers
- How to make customers recognise the fine service you give them
- The five best ways to keep customers coming back
- How to keep your customers happy

*How to Win Customers and Keep Them for Life* is a hard-hitting, action-ready, rewards and incentive programme for creating a winning sales team. Written by Michael LeBoeuf, one of America's foremost business consultants, this practical no-nonsense guide tells you everything you need to know about successful selling.